PRENTICE HALL INTERNATIONAL

Language Teaching Methodology Series

Teacher Education
General Editor: Christopher N. Candlin

Teaching and Learning Vocabulary

Other titles in this series include:

CANDLIN, Christopher and MURPHY, Dermot
Language learning tasks

ELLIS, Rod
Classroom language acquisition in context

ELLIS, Rod
Classroom second language development

FRANK, Christine and RINVOLUCRI, Mario
Grammar in action

KENNEDY, Chris
Language planning and English language teaching

KRASHEN, Stephen
Language acquisition and language education

KRASHEN, Stephen
Principles and practice in second language acquisition

KRASHEN, Stephen
Second language acquisition and second language learning

KRASHEN, Stephen and TERRELL, Tracy
The natural approach

MARTON, Waldemar
Methods in English language teaching: frameworks and options

McKAY, Sandra
Teaching grammar

NEWMARK, Peter
Approaches to translation

NUNAN, David
Understanding language classrooms

PECK, Antony
Language teachers at work

ROBINSON, Gail
Crosscultural understanding

STEVICK, Earl
Success with foreign languages

STEMPLESKI, Susan and TOMALIN, Barry
Video in action

SWALES, John
Episodes in ESP

WALLACE, Catherine
Learning to read in a multicultural society

WENDEN, Anita and RUBIN, Joan
Learner strategies in language learning

YALDEN, Janice
The communicative syllabus

Teaching and Learning Vocabulary

LINDA TAYLOR

ENGLISH LANGUAGE TEACHING

Prentice Hall

New York   London   Toronto   Sydney   Tokyo

First published 1990 by
Prentice Hall International (UK) Ltd
66 Wood Lane End, Hemel Hempstead
Hertfordshire HP2 4RG
A division of
Simon & Schuster International Group

Typeset in 10pt Times
by MHL Typesetting Ltd, Coventry

Printed and bound in Great Britain at the
University Press, Cambridge

Library of Congress Cataloging-in-Publication Data

Taylor, Linda (Linda L.)
    Teaching and learning vocabulary / Linda Taylor.
      p. cm. — (Language teaching methodology series)
    Includes bibliographical references.
    ISBN 0–13–895301–5: $10.95
    1. English language — Study and teaching — Foreign
speakers.
    2. Vocabulary — Study and teaching. I. Title. II. Series.
PE1128.A2T35 1990
428.2′4–dc20
                                    89-29106
                                        CIP

British Library Cataloguing in Publication data

Taylor, Linda
    Teaching and learning vocabulary. — (Language teaching
    methodology series. Teacher education).
    1. Educational institutions. Non-English speaking students
    I. Title II. Series
428.2′4

ISBN 0-13-895301-5

---

2 3 4 5 94 93 92

For my father, Sam

Contents

General Editor's Preface

Linda Taylor's new book for the Language Teaching Methodology Series appropriately enough targets *words* as being at the core of language teaching and learning. There was once an occasion in which second-language learners and teachers in some 'desert island' competition were asked what they would prefer to be marooned with, a grammar or a dictionary. The most popular answer (surprising to some) was the dictionary. It is not difficult to see why. Good dictionaries provide so much necessary information for the language learner: definitions, grammatical information, indications of usage, frequency, lexical structure and relationships, encyclopaedic information about culture and society. The most modern dictionaries, drawing on enormous databases of items, offer a picture of the state of the contemporary language unparalleled from any other source. So, *vocabulary* is central to language teaching and learning.

Dictionaries have drawbacks, however. They are not geared up to systematic teaching and learning. We need a pedagogically motivated way of encouraging the development of our learners' wordstores. Such a learner-centred methodology has to take into account both the context of the classroom and the contexts of out-of-classroom use. It needs to stress the gradual acquisition of the structure of vocabulary (its grammar, if you like) and its use in discourse. It has to take account of how vocabulary is learned and best retained; how learners can extend their store by astute listening to the words in context. Students need to learn and be taught judgement about vocabulary and its usage.

Accordingly, a book about teaching vocabulary cannot be restricted to issues of lexical structure, nor indeed to examples of words in discourse. It has to take the learner into account and in particular has to be sensitive to the major strides in the investigation of vocabulary acquisition which have taken place under the banner of studies in second-language research.

Just as vocabulary presents a challenge to learners to explore and extend their known worlds, so it does for the teacher. Linda Taylor has organised this book throughout on the basis of interpolating tasks and data for discussion and analysis, each example contributing to the overall objective of wording the learners' world. Not that her suggestions are for personal extension only; the book contains a wealth of practical suggestions for classroom practice, in keeping with the aims of the Language Teaching Methodology Series. Indeed, there are almost as many examples of conversations, written texts, computer printouts from databases, learners' and teachers' accounts, as there are structural, discoursal and pedagogic points about the nature of vocabulary and its teaching and learning. That is as it should be: the readership can use her ideas and their experience to construct together a rich and informed picture of this crucial topic for the language teacher and learner.

Professor Christopher N. Candlin
General Editor, Macquarie University, Sydney

Acknowledgements

My thanks are due to Mike McCarthy and to other staff at Birmingham University, who provided the impetus for this work; to colleagues and students at Eaton Hall International, who provided the data for my research; to Nottinghamshire County Council for granting me leave of absence for the same; to Bill Lee, who made encouraging comments about my first draft; and to my family for their constant support.

The publisher and author acknowledge with thanks the permission from the following to reproduce copyright material:

The BBC for extract from 'Medicine Now' (Radio 4, 5 April 1989)

Cambridge University Press for extracts from:
Gairns, R. and Redman, S., *Working with Words* (1986)
Swan, M. and Walter, C., *The Cambridge English Course I Practice Book* (1984)

W. and R. Chambers Ltd, Edinburgh for extracts from:
Chambers First Learners' Dictionary (1979)
Chambers Universal Learners' Dictionary Workbook (1981)

Cobuild Ltd for the extract from:
The Birmingham Collection of English Text: Cobuild, and the Research and Development Unit, University of Birmingham

Collins ELT for extracts from:
Collins Cobuild English Language Dictionary (1987)
Collins Cobuild Dictionary Diary (1989)
Sim, D. and Laufer-Dvorkin, B., *Vocabulary Development* (1984)

The *Daily Mail* Wednesday 5 April 1989

J. M. Dent and Everyman's Library for extract from:
Jones and Gimson, *Pronouncing Dictionary* 14th edn (1980)

Georgetown University Press for extract from:
Baily and Schuy (eds), *New Ways of Analyzing Variation in English* (1973)

The Guardian Wednesday 5 April 1989

Harrap Ltd for extracts from:
Winter, M., *Working With Your 2000 Word Dictionary* (1981)

Heinemann Educational Books Ltd for extracts from:
Grainger, C. and Beaumont, D., *New Generation I* (1986)
Wallace, M., *Teaching Vocabulary* (1982)

The Longman Group Ltd for extracts from:
Carter, R. and McCarthy, M., *Vocabulary and Language Teaching* (1988)
Harmer, J., *Meridian Activity Book I* (1985)
Longman Dictionary of Contemporary English
Longman Dictionary of Scientific Usage (1979)
Whitcut, J., *Learning with LDOCE* (1979)

Macmillan for extracts from:
Aston, P., 'Activity book' for *Up the Creek* (1985) in Hedge, T., below
Hedge, T., *Using Readers in Language Teaching* (1985)

Open University Press for extracts from:
Weiner, G. (ed.), *Just a Bunch of Girls* (1985)

Oxford University Press for extracts from:
Black, V. *et al.*, *Fast Forward* (1986)
Grellet, F. *et al.*, *Quartet Students' Book I* (1982)
Morgan, J. and Rinvolucri, M., *Vocabulary* (1986)
Oxford Elementary Learner's Dictionary of English (1981)
Viney, P., *Streamline English: Directions* (1985)

Penguin Books for extracts from:
Belgrave, R., *Way Ahead 2* (1986)
Harvey, P. and Walker, C., *Way Ahead 3* (1986)
Magness, C., *Way Ahead: Workbook 2* (1986)

The Times Wednesday 5 April 1989

Today Wednesday 5 April 1989

Unwin Hyman Ltd, for extract from:
Evans Learner's Dictionary of Science & Technology (1983)

Thanks are also due to David Brazil, Gwynneth Fox and Mario Rinvolucri

of a new vocabulary item, we should not expect our learners to be familiar with a connotation which we take for granted.

6. Knowledge of *polysemy*, i.e. knowing many of the different meanings associated with a word. For example, three meanings of 'still' are expressed in the following sentences:

I'm living in Retford now, but my father is *still* in London.
Stand *still* or I'll shoot.
A *still* is needed in the production of whisky.

One implication for teaching might be to ignore certain homographs at elementary level, if they are items of low frequency and likely to cause confusion. However, students are usually familiar with the problem in their own language, and enjoy finding several meanings for a single word. They often like to offer homographs themselves and are keen to clear up ambiguities. Many words exist in English which sound identical but which are spelt differently (and vice versa), so that it is important for us to teach the relationship of *sound and spelling*. Henning[7] has shown that when studying new vocabulary, elementary learners pay more attention to the acoustic factor, i.e. the sound of a word, than to the semantic, i.e. meaning. Low-proficiency learners do understand the meaning, but appear to encode words in memory on the basis of sound and spelling rather than by association of meaning. As proficiency increases, strategies of encoding vocabulary in memory change. This aspect of knowledge of a word is of particular relevance to learners unfamiliar with Roman script. One helpful suggestion, especially for elementary learners, is for the teacher to set new lexical items into the context of others of similar spelling or sound, such as 'mane', 'name', 'mean'.[8]

7. Knowledge of the equivalent of the word in the *mother tongue*. Use of the L1 used to be discouraged, but we now recognise the value of discussing and comparing how the same thing can be said in different languages. Banishing the mother tongue in the classroom diminishes its status, and in any case translation is bound to occur among students, especially in monolingual groups. If the teacher also knows the mother tongue of his students, translation will often save time. It is preferable to use the L1 and make a discussion point of difficulties, especially where there are 'false friends' or where there is no direct equivalent.

Sapir and Whorf[9] hypothesised that people do not have the same picture of the universe unless their linguistic backgrounds are the same. In its strong form, this hypothesis would lead us to the view that translation is impossible! However, we may well feel that, while possible, it is never wholly satisfactory.

How is it then that speakers of different languages arrive at common concepts? Fillmore[10] gives several notions of how meaning is understood: these include the concepts of 'prototype'[11] and of 'frame'. The 'prototype' is an object held to be very typical of the kind of object referred to by a given word: a robin is perhaps a more prototypical 'bird' than a penguin or an ostrich, whilst a 'squirrel' may be described as 'a funny looking cat'. The example of a 'frame' given by Fillmore is one which all people living within a money economy have in common, i.e. a 'commercial event': any one of many words such as 'buy', 'sell', 'pay', 'spend' that relate to this 'frame' is capable of activating a whole scene in our memory.

Another idea was put forward by Labov,[12] namely that we classify meanings into categories which have 'fuzzy' boundaries. For example, a 'cup' might be thought to have a set of essential features which make it 'cuppish', such as having a handle, having a saucer, holding liquid contents, being made of pottery. But how does 'cup' differ from 'bowl', 'mug', 'vase' or 'glass'? You could find out by gathering together a few friends (or learners) and trying the following experiment (based on Labov's own experiments).

1.3 Experiment: To establish that boundaries of word meanings are fuzzy

1. You will need to make cards, each showing one of the numbered 'cup-like objects' (see opposite). You can trace them singly on to card, or photocopy the set, cut out each one and paste on to card.

2. Find some willing 'victims' for your experiment: you will need at least four. Give each person a blank sheet of paper and *one* of the following instructions, which must not be revealed to the others:

    (a) You will be given a number of cards, one after the other. For each one, first write down on your sheet of paper the number of the object on the card. Look closely at the picture and give it a name. Write this name beside the number on your sheet of paper.

    (b) You will be given a number of cards, one after the other. For each one, write down the number of the object on the card. Now imagine it in someone's hand, being stirred with a spoon and having coffee drunk from it. Give the object a name, and write this name beside its number on your sheet of paper.

    (c) You will be given a number of cards, one after the other. For each one, first write down on your sheet of paper the number of the object on the card. Now imagine you are at a friend's house and this object is on the dinner table filled with rice or potatoes. Give the object a name, and write this name beside its number on your sheet of paper.

    (d) You will be given a number of cards, one after the other. For each one, first write down the number of the object on the card. Now imagine the object standing on a shelf with cut flowers in it. Give the object a name, and write this name beside its number on your sheet of paper.

3. Give out the cards, face downwards and one at a time, to the first person, who passes them on to the next, and so on. When everyone has named all the objects, discuss as a whole group any differences which emerge in the names they chose. You should find that (b) used the word 'cup' most frequently, that (c) used the word 'bowl' more frequently than the others, that (d) used the word 'vase' more frequently than the others, and that (a) showed a more varied number of names, as well as 'cup'.

Chapter 1

Words, Words, Words

1.1 How important is vocabulary?

> In order to live in the world, we must name it. Names are essential for the construction of reality for without a name it is difficult to accept the existence of an object, an event, a feeling. Naming is the means whereby we attempt to order and structure the chaos and flux of existence which would otherwise be an undifferentiated mass. By assigning names we impose a pattern and a meaning which allows us to manipulate the world.[1]

In foreign language teaching, vocabulary has for a long time been a neglected area. Pride of place has been given to 'structures' or, latterly, 'functions'. Course books have provided little guidance other than word lists, so that apart from turning to the specialised supplementary material, such as dictionary workbooks, teachers have been hard put to satisfy their students' demand for 'words'. Happily, this situation no longer obtains, and many of the newer course books include word study sections.[2] However. teachers still need to be aware of the methodologies available for introducing and consolidating new lexical items. Accordingly, this book describes practical techniques for both oral and written work on vocabulary, illustrated with lesson transcripts.

There are many contexts in which we may wish to minimise structural content and spend the greater part of our teaching time on lexis. For example, where students are learning the target language in the country in which that language is spoken, errors in syntax can be expected to disappear with time, and consequently more class time can be spent on vocabulary enrichment.[3] Another example would be an English for Specific Purposes (ESP) context where students are learning content through the target language.[4] Finally, vocabulary may have a special importance for adult learners, since it is the one area of language learning which does not appear to be slowed down by age.[5]

1.2 What does it mean to 'know' a word?

Knowledge of a word exists on various levels, which seem to be language universals. Many of these have been posited by Richards[6] and are set out briefly below:

1. Knowledge of the *frequency* of the word in the language, i.e. knowing the degree of probability of encountering the word in speech or in print. Some lexical items in English are far more frequent in speech than in writing, such as 'indeed', 'actually', 'well'. Other items, like 'former', 'latter', may only occur in the written language. One implication is that if we are teaching the target language in a country in which it is spoken, we may take it for granted that certain high-frequency vocabulary items

will be acquired outside the classroom and thus spend valuable class time on other items.

2. Knowledge of the *register* of the word, i.e. knowing the limitations imposed on the use of the word according to variations of function and situation. For example, 'Would you like a cigarette?' is a neutral formula, appropriate in most contexts. 'Want a fag?' may be an acceptable utterance between friends, but if made to a stranger it would be perceived as rude or insubordinate. One implication for teaching might be to introduce only neutral terms at elementary level in so far as this is possible, since these are capable of most generalisation.

3. Knowledge of *collocation*, both semantic and syntactic (sometimes termed colligation), i.e. knowing the syntactic behaviour associated with the word and also knowing the network of associations between that word and other words in the language. For example, the word 'overtake' is a verb, normally transitive, likely to be used in active voice, and followed by article + noun, or pronoun. It is moreover likely to occur in the context of transport, in the vicinity of items such as 'lane', 'car', 'speed'. One implication for teaching would be to ensure that we do not merely teach new items of vocabulary in isolation, but give a meaningful context for the word, if possible with several examples of its use in connected discourse. To help foster a knowledge of the network of associations between words we can use *hyponyms* or *superordinates*. For example, 'raspberry' and 'strawberry' are hyponyms of 'fruit'. 'Fruit' is also the *superordinate* term for 'gooseberry', 'apple', 'blackcurrant'. Such classifications may not be common to every culture or language, and interesting discussion can develop, e.g. as to whether a tomato is a fruit!

4. Knowledge of *morphology*, i.e. knowing the underlying form of a word and the derivations that can be made from it. For example, the word 'dissatisfaction' has a common prefix denoting opposite (dis-), a common noun suffix (-ion) and is derived from the verb 'satisfy'. One implication for teaching is that we should not be shy of pointing out relationships between parts of speech having a common root. Knowledge of morphological patterns facilitates understanding in a way analogous to knowledge of multiplication tables in mathematics.

5. Knowledge of *semantics*, i.e. knowing firstly what the word means or 'denotes'. It is relatively easy to teach denotation of concrete items like 'plate', 'ruler' or 'banana' by simply bringing these objects (realia), or pictures of these objects, into the classroom. For more abstract concepts, *synonyms, paraphrases* or *definitions* may be useful. *Antonyms* are also important, since it is necessary to know what a word does *not* mean as well as what it does mean. Semantic knowledge involves knowing secondly what the word 'connotes'. For example, in Western culture the word 'slim' is positively evaluated, whilst we have many euphemisms for the negatively evaluated term 'fat', such as 'plump', 'portly' or 'well-built'. However, 'You've put on weight' may be perceived as a compliment in some cultures. An implication of all this for teaching may be that while we may devote time to teaching the more obvious *de*notation

Variations

1. You might find there are rather too many cards to cope with. In that case, choose a smaller number of objects taken at random from the set.
2. If there are non-native speakers of English in the group, you could ask them to name the objects in their native language, for comparison. You could also translate their instructions into their mother tongue.

1.4   Is L2 vocabulary learning like L1 vocabulary learning?

Many insights into L2 learning have been gained through studies of how we learn our native language. It is sometimes held that children 'acquire' language in an informal way whereas adults may also 'learn' language by conscious application of rules.[13] Whether in fact children do 'learn' as well as 'acquire' is still open to question, but the distinction is useful for us in the teaching of vocabulary: we can provide 'learning' type activities by discussing the *formal* aspect of a new vocabulary item, focusing on it and encouraging its repetition by activities such as work on definitions, affixes or pronunciation, and follow this up with freer 'acquisition' type activities in which the new item is used in *meaningful interaction*. In any case repetition is a prominent feature both of mother—child interaction and of native to non-native discourse. In the former the mother makes frequent repetitions of her own utterances in order to continue the conversation, whereas in the latter the main motivation for repetition comes from the native speaker's desire to clarify the foreigner's misunderstandings. Such repetitions may not be exact, but often involve paraphrase, synonyms or expansion.

Mother—child discourse ('motherese') and native to non-native discourse ('foreigner-talk') also have in common a simplified register which varies according to the proficiency of the learner.[14] As language teachers, we quite naturally display an effort to use only basic vocabulary and to approximate our language, both syntactically and phonologically, to the 'standard', in our case received pronunciation (RP) and Southern British Standard (SBS).[15]

Furthermore, in child—adult discourse the adult does not suggest topics of which the child has no background information. In teaching non-native speakers, then, we might introduce new vocabulary into the context of what our learners already know, culturally as well as linguistically.

Finally, mothers do not normally correct the grammar of what their children say, but they do correct content (Example 1). This seems also to be the case in naturally occurring native to non-native conversation, as the following transcript (Example 2) shows. However, we can see that in both the following transcripts grammar is covertly 'corrected' by means of expansion, reformulation, or a question to ascertain what was intended. The new vocabulary items being 'acquired', since both situations are informal, are italicised in the transcripts, and a discussion follows of the teachers' (the mother, too, is included here) methods. This discussion is related to the aspects of 'knowing a word' above.

EXAMPLE 1[16]

Key: M = Mother; C = Child. Phonetic transcription is used only where no recognisable English word is spoken.
C: There. A man there. There. A man there. See there də man.
M: A man?
C: Yes.
M: What's that?
C: Its də man. də man. It stand up. It stand up.
M: It stands up, does it? Can you find a hat for that one?

C: Yes. ... No want that. Two got ones. Two got ones.
M: Mmm?
C: Two got ones.
M: You got two?
C: Yes. Got one you. This one and *back* one. And *back* one.
M: *Black* one.
C: Yes. I got three.
M: You got three?
C: Yes. Now I got three. Got three now. That one.
M: How many have you got now? You count.
C: 's də *back*. hizə *back*. hiz *back*.
M: Put that one *back*?
C: *Black*.
M: Oh *black*.
C: That one.
M: What colour's that?
C: Red.
M: Red? No it isn't. Is it red?
C: No.
M. What is it?
C: Lellow.
M: No. It's green.
C: Green?
M:　Mmm.

EXAMPLE 2[17]

Key: T = Teacher; S = Student.
S: Yes yes er no she is do er daughter *nephew, nephew.*
T: *Nephew.*
S: His her sister, yes her *nephew*, yes her sister, her sister daughter.
T: Her sister's daughter.
S: *Nephew*, yes yes in the Police.
T: Oh, her sister's son was in the Secret Police, or Civil Service.
S: Her sister's son, yes.
S: Government, what you call this, MIF?
T: Civil Service? *MI5*?
S: Yes, this one.
T: Was he in *MI5*?
S: Yes.
T: Ah.
S: Shipboard, I think.
T: And she had some information, did she?
S: Yes.

Comment

In Example 1, the item 'black' is being familiarised, and in Example 2 'nephew' and 'MI5'. In all cases, the learners have some inkling as to the item they need, but the teacher does not find it adequate for her own comprehension. In Example 1 the first utterance of *back* is understood correctly as *black*. However, the second occurrence of the item is ambiguous because the preceding words are also unclear. The teacher/mother checks what is meant by asking a question made up of what she supposes to be a reformulation of the child's intended utterance. In response, the child is able to articulate *black* correctly, having previously heard the mother do so, and this is reinforced by the mother's repetition.

The 'lesson' here is thus a knowledge of the phonology of the word, by in effect using the minimal pair *back/black* to point out that misunderstanding can occur if *black* is mispronounced.

In Example 2, the aspect of 'knowledge of a word' being taught for *nephew* is the one I have listed under no. 5 above, concerned with semantics. The student gives a definition of *nephew* as *sister daugher* and thus confuses his teacher until mention is made of the Police, so that she assumes the person in question to be male, and thus the *sister's son* instead. The amount of repetition here, as in the previous transcript, is noteworthy. The same is true of the second item, *MI5*. The teacher is not certain that her explanation is correct, so checks learning by asking a question formulated to include the item she thinks is required. The positive response from the student then indicates that the item needed was in fact *MI5*. As in Example 1, it is the phonology of the item which is being familiarised.

In these extracts of naturally occurring interaction, utterances which are erroneous but do not interfere with communication are allowed to pass. These include, in Example 1, *No want that* and *Lellow*, and in Example 2 *Shipboard I think*. Other erroneous utterances are 'corrected' covertly by reformulation, with or without questioning intonation. These are: *It stands up does it?* (correcting third person sigular -s) and *you got two* (correcting word order) in Example 1, and *Her sister's daughter* (correcting apostrophe + s genitive) in Example 2. It is only the error in content, *red* and *lellow* instead of *green*, which is overtly corrected. There are implications here for teaching 'acquisition' by using fluency practice to reinforce items previously 'taught', though perhaps imperfectly understood.

1.5 Tasks

Group tasks

1. Look at the following examples of how the word 'matter' is used in English, from the *Collins Cobuild Dictionary*:

    (a) A matter is an event, situation or subject which you have to deal with or think about, especially one that involves problems, e.g.:
    'It was a purely personal matter'
    'Will you report the matter to the authorities?'
    'The House of Commons is due to debate the matter'

   (b) Matter is written material, especially books and newspapers, e.g.:
      'Their reading matter included *The Voyages of Captain Cook*'
      'He read everything, even the advertising matter in books of stamps'
   (c) Matter is the physical part of the universe consisting of solids, liquids and gases,
      e.g.:
      'An atom is the smallest indivisible particle of matter'
      'My research is concerned with the way matter behaves at the very lowest
      temperatures'
   (d) You say 'It doesn't matter' to tell someone who is apologising to you that you
      are not angry or upset, or when someone offers you a choice between two or
      more things and you do not mind which is chosen, e.g.:
      'I've only got dried milk.' — 'It doesn't matter'
      'Do you want your coffee black?' — 'It doesn't matter'

Discuss which meanings you think are the most frequent. Decide on more examples
which would show your learners the appropriate register and collocations for this word.
How would you translate the above examples in your mother tongue?
2.   Discuss the pronunciation of the word 'matter'. Can this vary? How would your
     learners pronounce it? How could you correct their pronunciation?
3.   Chapter 1, Example 2, shows learners acquiring the item 'nephew'. Devise an activity
     or exercise to reinforce this initial familiarisation in a more formal way.
4.   Discuss the morphology of the word 'matter'. Is it always a noun? Can you think
     of other words ending in -er? How do they behave in a sentence? For your chosen
     words, can you remove the -er ending and still have a word? Can you also add another
     ending on to the -er and still have a word?

Self-assessed tasks

1.   Arrange the following lexical items in order of their frequency in spoken English:
     whether
     certainly
     whatever
     exactly
     absolutely
     well
     obviously
2.   Make pairs of phrases with similar meaning, and say which is the more formal in
     each pair:
     He passed away
     Put a sock in it
     I should get a bigger one, if I were you
     It was absolutely bucketing down
     He kicked the bucket
     Don't move

I advise you to buy the next size up
You are requested to remain seated
There was torrential rain
Could I ask you to make a little less noise?

3. Classify these activities into three groups and give each group of words a heading:
    cycling
    cleaning floors
    jogging
    washing dishes
    sewing
    stamp collecting
    making beds
    bird watching
    walking in the mountains

4. Which of these are 'noun suffixes' and which are 'verb suffixes'?
    -tion -ment -ness -ic -our -ful -ive -al

5. Which of these pairs of words can rhyme, and which cannot?

    cough   tough
    bow   so
    heard   bird
    bare   tear
    arithmetic anaesthetic
    bother   another

6. Classify the extracts below according to whether they illustrate formal instruction ('learning') or natural interaction ('acquisition'):

(a)

> T: (showing picture of eagle) What is it covered in? Is it covered in hair?
> S$_1$: No, no.
> S$_2$: (Arabic translation)
> T: Ah, this is in Arabic, what is it in English?
> SS: (word search: discussion in L1 and L2)
> T: (writes first three letters slowly) What is it?
> S$_3$: Feth...
> T: Feth... (writes rest of word)
> S$_2$: fɛðiər.
> S$_1$: *Feather.*
> S$_3$: *Feather*
> T: It's covered in *feathers.*

(b)

> T: Do you know any of the animals in Australia? Do you know the one that jumps about with a long tail?
> S: Yes, special...er kango, kangour.
> T: Kango...
> S: Kango, kangouri.
> T: *Kangaroo*, yes *kangaroo, kangaroo*.

(c)

> S₁: They got the diver men coming inside the water and take the camera and the light.
> T: Oh the *frogmen* went down did they?
> S₂: Yes the *frogmen* yes.
> S₁: *Frogmen*.
> S₃: But I think that's not come inside the body.
> S₂: I think no maybe somebody is trick.
> T: She wasn't there, they couldn't find the body.
>
> — — —
>
> T: ...and nobody could find her...three months, she's been missing for three months...and did they have many Policemen there behind the telephones ready to...
> S₂: Yes er helicopter, plane, and er dogs, and the *frogmen* and er some er many people is go to there from the Police.
> T: But they couldn't find her.

(d)

> T: (holding up picture) What shall we give her?
> S₁: Oh (L1)
> T: Mmm...Let's give her some...
> S₂: Pen, pen.
> T: *Lipstick*.
> S₁: *Lipstick*.
> T: Pen for the lips. *Lipstick*.
> S₂: *Lipstick*.
> T: Let's give her some *lipstick*. (writes on board)

(e)

T: She came over to England to learn English.

S₁: English.

S₂: To learn English and she is can't speak English, can't speak English speaking with Ara...with French.

T: Yes.

S₂: ...with France and one day is go to the sightseeing in the weekend, take some er clothes and some things in er in ba...in bag her back er...

T: She had a *backpack*.

S₂: *Bagpack*.

T: Yes.

S₂: ...and er go to that, where, Yousef?

T: Where did she go? In the country, or to a town or...

S₁: No in the country.

— — —

T: And now they've found the body, they've connected him.

S₂: Yes found the body yes and her bag her backpack that's her bag bag er *backpack* for that lady's before was in the lack.

T: And did they find the French girl?

S₁: No.

T: No they didn't find the body.

S₂: No don't find.

Notes and References

1. The opening quotation is from D. Spender, *Man Made Language*, Routledge & Kegan Paul, 1980, p.163.

2. I have used examples from some of these as illustrations for this book. Most course books tackle vocabulary teaching alongside the main syllabus of the course book which is usually structural, functional or situational. I would refer readers to the Teacher's Books of D. Willis and J. Willis, *The Cobuild English Course*, for an account of how a syllabus graded according to vocabulary (the so-called lexical syllabus) works.

3. E. L. Judd, 'Vocabulary teaching and TESOL: A need for re-evaluation of existing assumptions', *TESOL Quarterly* 1978, **12(1)**: 71−6.

4. M. Saville-Troike, 'What really matters in second language learning for academic achievement?', *TESOL Quarterly* 1984, **18(2)**: 199−219.

5. W. Rivers, *Communicating Naturally in a Foreign Language*, Oxford University Press, 1983.

6. J. Richards, 'The role of vocabulary teaching', *TESOL Quarterly* 1976, **10(1)**: 77−90.

7. G. H. Henning, 'Remembering foreign language vocabulary: Acoustic and semantic parameters', *Language Learning* 1973, **23(2)**: 185−95.

8. M. Donley, 'The role of structural semantics in expanding and activating the vocabulary of the advanced learner; the example of the homophone', *Audio-visual Language Journal* 1974, **12(2)**: 81−9.

9. I would refer the reader to J. B. Carroll (ed.), *Language, Thought and Reality*, and in particular to Benjamin Whorf's article therein, 'An American Indian Model of the Universe'.

10. C. J. Fillmore, 'Frame semantics and the nature of language', *Annals of the New York Academy of Sciences* 1976, **280**: 20–32.

11. Recent work on 'prototypes', a word coined by Ludwig Wittgenstein, has been done by Eleanor Rosch, whose article 'Natural categories', *Cognitive Psychology* **4**: 328–50, is referred to here by Fillmore.

12. W. Labov, 'The boundaries of words and their meanings' in Bailey and Schuy (eds.), *New Ways of Analyzing Variation in English*, Georgetown University School of Language & Linguistics, 1973.

13. Stephen Krashen explains his so-called 'Monitor Theory' in various of his works. I would refer the reader to *Principles and Practice in Second Language Acquisition* (Prentice Hall, 1982), *Second Language Acquisition and Second Language Learning* (Prentice Hall, 1981) and to ch. 2 of Barry McLaughlin's *Theories of Second Language Learning* (Edward Arnold, 1987).

14. B. Freed, 'Foreigner talk, baby talk, native talk', *International Journal of the Sociology of Language* 1981, **23**: 19–39.

15. Received pronunciation and Southern British Standard are accepted as the standard accent and dialect of British English.

16. Example 1 is taken from a transcript of a recording of a conversation between myself and my second son, Zephan, then aged 2.4 years.

17. Example 2 and all succeeding extracts from classroom interaction are from lessons given at Eaton Hall International. (Thank you Esther, Mary, Sue, David, Des and John.)

Chapter 2

The Communicative Teaching of Vocabulary: Presenting New Items

2.1 How should I present new vocabulary?

When we work on a reading or listening comprehension, we may wish to pre-teach items of vocabulary which are likely to cause difficulties. We can do so by *pre-familiarisation* or by *post-familiarisation*.[1]

Pre-familiarisation is a technique for establishing 'sense' first by encouraging students to attend to the topic, then moving on to 'item', as in Example 3 below:

EXAMPLE 3

T: What do you call the special big shoes that come up to here for...em...when it's snowing?

S: Er...

T: Not shoes, but...

S: *Boots*.

Post-familiarisation is the opposite process where 'item' is given before 'sense', as in Example 4 below:

EXAMPLE 4

T: *In fact*. Do you know what that means?

S: *In fact*.

T: *In fact*. Really.

All the items in the transcripts in Chapter 1 were thus post-familiarised.

2.1.1 *Using a written stimulus*

This lends itself to the technique of post-familiarisation. The learners are first presented with the 'item', in its graphological representation, and try their best to work out for themselves the 'sense':

14

EXAMPLE 5

S: *Religious* (reading)
T: *Religious*?
S: Yes.
T: Er...'*Religious* festival'. Now your National Day in Oman is not a *religious* festival, but Id is a *religious* festival. A *religious* festival is something to do with what you believe, your God. Right? It's something to do with Mohammed or with...er...Abraham...and that's Id, isn't it? But your National Day is just a National festival, it's not to do with the Koran...
S: Yes, yes.
T: *Religious*, yes.
S: *Religious*.
T: What are your *religious* festivals, Id al Fitre?
S: Id al Fitre and Haj.
T: Ah another one.
S: And Mohammed immigration...Mohammed immigrate...migration.

Although post-familiarisation is the norm with a written stimulus, there are techniques for pre-familiarisation. In Example 6, the written word is used in conjunction with a non-verbal stimulus (a magazine picture). While students try hard to recall the item, it is written letter by letter on the board.

EXAMPLE 6

(Phonetic script is used where word is not recognisable.)

T: (showing picture of eagle) What is it covered in? Is it covered in hair?
S$_1$: No, no.
S$_2$: (Arabic translation)
T: Ah, this is in Arabic, what is it in English?
SS: (word search: discussion in L1 and L2)
T: (writes first three letters slowly) What is it?
S$_3$: Feth...
T: Feth... (writes rest of word)
S$_2$: fɛðiər.
S$_1$: *Feather*.
S$_3$: *Feather*.
T: It's covered in *feathers*.

2.1.2 *Using a non-verbal stimulus*

Just as a written stimulus lends itself to *post*-familiarisation, so a non-verbal stimulus is more suited to *pre*-familiarisation. The 'sense' is established to encourage a word search, followed by 'item'. Example 7 shows the technique using a magazine picture stimulus, and Example 8 shows the same technique using realia:

EXAMPLE 7

T: What kind of coat is it? (shows picture of fur coat)
S: White.
T: White yes, what kind of material?
S: Cotton, cotton.
T: Oh it's not cotton is it?
S: Wool.
T: It's not really wool. Em...em...
S: Material.
T: Material yes. It's the kind of...
S: Sof or soft...
T: Animal. What...er animal skin, isn't it?
S: Frer. Furr.
T: *Fur.* Have you heard that before? I'll write it up on the board.
S: (reads) *Fur* coat.

EXAMPLE 8

T: (holds up tablet) And what about this tablet. What do you think that's for?
S: Backache maybe.
T: No, it's not backache.
S: Stomach.
T: Not my stomach. This is a bit hard. It's a *vitamin* tablet actually.

Very often a pre-familiarisation can be followed up and consolidated by post-familiarisation, as in Example 7, where the item is written and then pronunciation practice follows.

2.1.3 *Using an oral/aural stimulus*

This is most versatile, being equally well suited to pre- and post-familiarisation. Pre-familiarisation occurs in Example 9 and post-familiarisation in Example 10.

EXAMPLE 9

> T: Do you know any of the animals in Australia? Do you know the one that jumps about with a long tail?
> S: Yes, special...er kango, kangour.
> T: Kanga...
> S: Kanga, kangouri.
> T: *Kangaroo*, yes *kangaroo, kangaroo*.

EXAMPLE 10

> T: Antelope. (repeating item on tape cassette) An antelope is...like a gazelle.
> S: Ah.

It is interesting that oral/aural pre- and post-familiarisation occur naturally all the time in native and non-native discourse but such items are glossed over, being mere hiccups in communication. They are dealt with fleetingly, with no overt markers such as 'it means...' or 'it's like a...'. In natural conversation there is no written consolidation, nor much repetition. Compare Examples 11 and 12:

EXAMPLE 11

> S: But they put it er £33,000 when they anybody catch it.
> T: Oh there's a *reward*.
> S: Yes, but it's not enough.

EXAMPLE 12

> T: Do you let the *public* into your courts or not, or just the people in the case? Can the people come in from outside...

2.1.4 Recommendations for use of stimuli

In order to give learners as wide a knowledge as possible of an item, a combination of stimuli is desirable, with written consolidation for adults, in order to facilitate transfer from short-term to long-term memory. Example 13 shows the maximum combination of stimuli, with both pre- and post-familiarisation. The latter part of the extract shows the importance of giving learners time to assimilate.

EXAMPLE 13

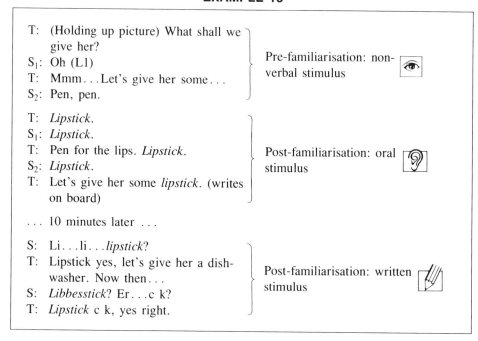

T: (Holding up picture) What shall we give her?
S₁: Oh (L1)
T: Mmm...Let's give her some...
S₂: Pen, pen.

⎫ Pre-familiarisation: non-verbal stimulus

T: *Lipstick.*
S₁: *Lipstick.*
T: Pen for the lips. *Lipstick.*
S₂: *Lipstick.*
T: Let's give her some *lipstick.* (writes on board)

⎫ Post-familiarisation: oral stimulus

... 10 minutes later ...

S: Li...li...*lipstick?*
T: Lipstick yes, let's give her a dishwasher. Now then...
S: *Libbesstick?* Er...c k?
T: *Lipstick* c k, yes right.

⎫ Post-familiarisation: written stimulus

Let's now return to our seven aspects of 'knowledge of a word' for fuller discussion and illustration.

2.2 Frequency

Vocabulary items of high frequency and neutrality form a 'core' vocabulary[2] (sometimes termed 'procedural' vocabulary).[3] For example, the item 'people', although it is an irregular plural form and difficult to spell, is one whose denotation I have never had to 'teach'. The following extracts show how a student acquired this word merely through repeated procedural use:

EXAMPLE 14

Lesson 1: T: Retford is nice, I like it, but maybe for young *people*...
Lesson 2: S: But all the *person, pupil* is understand what you mean...
Lesson 5: S: The *people* is coming from outside to inside the court...
Lesson 8: S: Some *people*, Bedous or people from Gulf, is use it...

However, some items of high frequency, whose denotation does not cause problems, nevertheless have attendant syntax which may be difficult to master. 'Same' and 'different' are two such, and learners will need to be taught holistically 'Is it the same as. . .?', 'Is is different from. . .', 'Is it like. . .?' so that they can make clear requests for clarification if the need arises.

The metafunction of naming is perhaps present only in the context of a language course. Nevertheless the verb 'to call' in phrases like 'In my language we call it. . .' or 'It's called. . .' is much more common than its other sense of 'to shout' in the context of language teaching. Some textbook writers have recognised the need to teach common classroom vocabulary which, though not particularly frequent in the language as a whole, is very prominent in an educational context − as demonstrated in Example 15.

EXAMPLE 15

C Classroom language

1 🔘🔘

Listen and fill in the blanks.

a
A: Excuse me, Mr Smith, how _____ _____ pronounce this word in English?
B: 'Lecturer.'
A: What _____ it mean?
B: A college teacher.
A: Oh, I see. Thank you.

b
A: Um . . . I _____ understand. Could you explain the difference between 'school' and 'college'?
B: A college _____ usually for students over sixteen.
A: Oh, I understand now. Thank you.

c
A: How _____ _____ say that _____ _____ English?
B: The English word _____ 'register'.
A: _____ _____ _____ spell it?
B: R–E–G–I–S–T–E–R.
A: Could you repeat that, please?
B: R–E–G–I–S–T–E–R.
A: Thanks.

In illustration, speech bubbles: 'school' ? 'college' ?   regester? register? ngester?

2
Look at this:

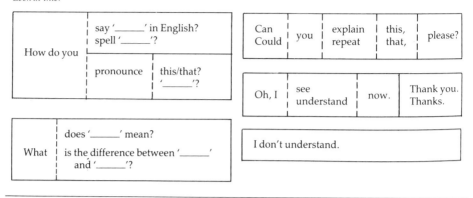

The following extracts (Example 16) from EFL classes show how teacher explanations utilise 'core' vocabulary:

EXAMPLE 16

Nylon. Explanation: Not proper fur; made by man in a factory.
Heat.   Explanation: Heat from the sun...hot and cold from the sun.
Doll.   Explanation: Something to look like a man.

One of the most exciting developments of recent years is the possibility, through the use of computers, of accessing vast amounts of authentic English text, both spoken and written. Such computer-based studies reveal not only the most frequently occurring English words, but also their behaviour in sentences or utterances. For example, the ten most frequent words of English (see Example 17a) account for 23 per cent of all English text;

EXAMPLE 17a

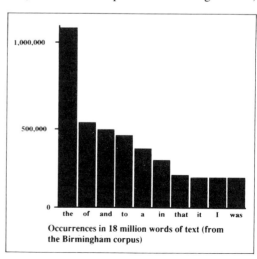

Occurrences in 18 million words of text (from the Birmingham corpus)

EXAMPLE 17b

Ref	Reg	Left context	Key	Right context
GW0081	BR	I was eighteen months old at the time. There had	obviously	been nannies before that, but I either h
GS0048	BR	g one or two beautifully carved tables which had	obviously	been carved by an individual spending q
GS0050		must be more or less guess work, although you've	obviously	been up there and you must have found o
GS0101		be changed – Hmmm. mm – But you see nothing had	obviously	been done at all – They, you see, were
GS0101	BR	matter of fact the stair I was in on Friday had	obviously	been used as a lavatory, we were ... er
GS0122	BR	as.... and then it's ob- the state boundary had	obviously	been done by a draughtsman using a rule
GW0069	BR	s hardily w? orth bothering with someone so <P 63>	obviously	beneath your notice. It is. This girl is
GW0026	AU	ut that right when we took direct rule but it had	obviously	bitten very deep. ((SW)) Can I just int
GW0019	AM	I was wondering where I'd picked up this piece of	obviously	blatant misinformation for she suddenly
GW0055	BR	aconically chortling to itself and who was by now	obviously	bored, flew across to the tree and aligh
GS0059	BR	ld be any hope of overcoming the toubob, who were	obviously	both well organized and heavily armed. A
GS0098		(DC)) Well, it's a question of defective consent,	obviously	but the doctor, I think, ought ordinar
GS0124		and forced, I can get away with that sometimes,	obviously	but, you know – I thought you just a
GS0124		ou inherit a class, you have your module system,	obviously	but they come to expect a fluidity, an
GW0143	BR	f. Her flat voice angered him. "I may as well.	obviously	but you will inherit a group, a new gr
GW0052	BR	ead the information the African section must	obviously	can't please you." "Of course you please
GW0055	AM	has it raced for cov in the tall grass. He was	obviously	cease. If the leaks continued there coul
GW0081	BR	pace far more often than poor housing conditions.	Obviously	chasing it for sport rather than for foo
GS0001		best way of playing it. But one question that has	obviously	children from large families, particular
GS0057		e, from a certain social class. Occupationally, I	obviously	come up in a lot of people's minds, is t
GW0067	AM	at on earth shops do during week if entire county	obviously	come from a certain kind of social clas
GS0002	BR	oncoming traffic they see some fair distance away	obviously	comes Saturday morning? Long queue at sp
GS0019	BR	he relationship between State and Party. Leninism	obviously	coming out of line coming the other way
GS0144	BR	nd of the Second World War two major powers, one	obviously	commends itself to a militant labour lea
GW0006	AM	ou well. ((RM)) Very well. ((LB)) But you haven't	obviously	completely outside Europe – the United S
GW0063	AM	bens's plump nudes, with their many dimples, were	obviously	concentrated itself on Japan with your own hol
GS0046		r to the first bedroom. There were two beds, each	obviously	considered beautiful. It seems to be ha
GW0043	BR	h pregnancy testing in..in cous (l. Uh huh), and	obviously	containing only one person; He closed th
GW0065		fis not thereby freed from responsibility but is	obviously	cows are the <P 90> economic (um)...of e
GW0063	AM	e thing. And the edges are too perfect. They were	Obviously	crime is going to be squeezed in a varie
GW0081	BR	ent might not," said Rosemary Haughton. They were	obviously	culpable. We are just as re- sponsible f
GW0056	AM	f them–both the butches and the femmes–had <P 55>	obviously	cut." "I suppose you could send them bac
GS0034		act. A very strange john it is, too, a large room	obviously	dangers of missing individual attention.
GW0039	BR	s gave him an opportunity to weigh them; which he	obviously	decided to take up homosexuality during
GW0117	OT	's that? "Well it's like this, Chief .((MM)) Well	obviously	decisions that have to be made, policies
GW0144	BR	rom your husband's. How did you do. ((MM)) Well I	obviously	designed originally for some other purpo
GW0043	BR	e biological central nervous system may not be so	obviously	did, for he grew thoughtful and his mood
GW0119	BR	or three wives and four or five strong sons will	obviously	didn't want to go into details. Brody he
GW0062	BR	did you get that thing on the mantelpiece? (She	obviously	didn't do very well. And I made the mis
GS0089		a <3,000 M> school system in this country, which	obviously	digital, though there is evidence that
GS0117	BR	s they spoke. A child who squirms in his chair is	obviously	disagree," says Howard, "you keep your B
GW0078	OT	also a Professor of English at Sussex. Tony, we	obviously	do well for himself. But his sons will
GW0081	BR	es a kind of awe, inferiority does not, and it is	obviously	does not want to wait for an answer.) Wh
GW0077	BR	milies and raise them with amazing success. It is	obviously	doesn't offer equality to children. I m
GW0013	BR	constitutional monarch is the dollar. Not really.	obviously	don't want to interfere with the interna
GW0056	BR	has requested a suit for himself. He said it was	obviously	dying to escape and any parent recognize
GW0081	BR	he was Black like all the rest of us, the cop was	obviously	easier to treat the inferior man kindly
GS0046		y thought they'd really got something.' There ca	obviously	easier if the parents are rich enough to
		ficult medium t? o measure ac...accurately. (Um)	obviously	economic forces rule. But in England the
GS0140	BR	he last 20 years. Er, which doesn't mean to say.	obviously	embarrassing for clergymen to have to as
GW0056	AM	Tombs had erupted in massive collective protests.	Obviously	embarrassed. He worked off his embarrass
GS0134	BR	h which it should wish to associate itself, most	obviously	emotional problems too, which are greate
			obviously	(er) noise has to be broken into. its com
			obviously	er, that I've been concerned with one
			obviously	every prison in New York was searching
			obviously	evidently in such things like the Garde

yet frequent words are the very ones that native speakers of English never pause to consider, let alone teach. The computer may have surprises in store for us if we study these closely.[5] Computer programs have been designed which show separate lines of text, each from a different source in the data bank, in such a way that the vocabulary item to be studied is always aligned in the centre of the page, as in Example 17b.[6] Lines like these are known as 'concordances'. Since the commonest and most important *meanings* in English are those expressed by the commonest *words* in English, we can use computer concordances to specify these words, identify their meanings and discover their patterns of occurrence.[7] Sixty-nine per cent of all the English language we produce and receive is expressed by the 700 most frequent words of English. These 700 words, graded according to their frequency in authentic discourse, might form – and indeed *have* formed[7] – the syllabus of a course book for elementary learners of English. Such a grading system allows exposure, from beginner level, to 'real' language rather than to the scripted and simplified language of most course books in which, for example, the past tense of the verb to be (cf. Example 17a, which shows 'was' among the ten most frequent English words) may not appear until its two present tenses have been introduced. Moreover, with a grading based on authentic language, learners should find a better match between the English they are taught in school and the English they encounter on their first visit to Britain!

2.3 Register

Increasing access, via computerised word lists, to actual instances of vocabulary in use, has emphasised the important relationship between frequency and register. For example, in the incomplete phrase 'Look forward to...you' we not do have an infinite choice of verbs from which to fill the empty slot. While 'Look forward to seeing you' or 'Look forward to hearing from you' may seem acceptable, 'Look forward to clapping eyes on you' does not.[9] Items of high frequency tend to occur together, just as items of low frequency do, as Examples 18 and 19 respectively show. The numbers above the vocabulary items refer to the estimated level of difficulty of each according to *The Cambridge English Lexicon*,[10] but crosses show that the items so marked do not occur in the *Lexicon*, being of too high a level of difficulty.

EXAMPLE 18


```
              4        2            3   1              4
'It's not that insurance companies don't trust students to be good drivers. It's
       2
not a case of trusting them at all, it's a case of their finding students to be the
   2     4
biggest risk.'
```

EXAMPLE 19

---

                         x   1   4   x   x   x

'The kitchen was small, compact, clean, a minor culinary symphony in stainless

 3   5

steel and white tiles.'

(Both the above examples are from naturally occurring discourse.[11] We should try to avoid the kind of manipulative exercise which requires substitution of one lexical item for another of a different level of frequency, e.g. substituting 'get' with other verbs: only unnatural language will result; see Example 20.)

EXAMPLE 20

Substitute another word for 'get' each time it appears in the following text:

'For Christmas this year we got a video recorder. At first we couldn't get it to work because one of the buttons kept getting stuck, but now we've got used to it and we've taped a lot of programmes. We've got all the Superman films on tape too.'

The teaching of register is best done using a 'functional' approach. For example, to teach the function of disagreeing many exponents are available, such as 'You've got to be joking', 'Oh come on!', 'That's absolute rubbish', 'Well I wouldn't say that exactly', 'I'm not sure I'd agree with you on that one'. Discussion can then ensue on a plausible context for each and on the likely relationship between the participants in the discourse. It has to be said that this aspect of knowledge of a word is best left until learners have achieved a certain competence in the language!

2.4 Collocation

Example 21 shows the use of hyponymy.

EXAMPLE 21

T: And we have a special name, a special name . . . what do you call an animal that gives the baby milk?

S: Cows.

T: Cows.

S: Camels.

T: Camels.

S: Cats.

T: Cats.

S: Goats.
T: Goats.
S: Sheep.
T: Sheep. We have a name for these animals, special name... (writes)
S: (reads) *Mammal.*

The four extracts in Example 22 illustrate the other aspect of collocation, i.e. knowing the syntactic behaviour associated with the word.

EXAMPLE 22

(a) T: *Landing*, it's in fact the hall upstairs...
     S: Yes, *landing*.
     S: Fire *landing.*

(b) T: So you can get a record *token*, gift *token*, or er book *token.*

(c) T: Can you *change* round, *change* roles, change em...

(d) T: He has a camera, he's a photographer.
     S: Yes.
     T: He is *interested* in...
     S: Photographer.
     T: Photography. He is *interested* in photography.
     S: He is interesting photography.
     T: He is *interested* in photography.
     S: He is *interested* photography.
     T: In photography.
     S: In photography.

2.5 Morphology

Many teachers are shy of exploiting this aspect orally, because of a fear that to do so would be to talk 'about' the language rather than to 'use' it. Happily for teachers, this decade has seen the pendulum of methodology trends swing back from an exclusively inductive approach towards an acceptance of overt grammatical explanations whenever they save time. In any case, attention to the morphological aspect of knowledge of a word does not necessarily involve explanation 'about' the language, as Example 23 shows:

EXAMPLE 23

S: Very *bored*.

T: Very *bored*. Very *bored*. What about the other man, what do you think about him?

S: A little *bored*.

T: Look at those two. Are they *bored*?

S: No. Happy.

T: They are happy. For them life is exciting or *boring*?

S: Exciting.

T: Life is exciting. Certainly not *boring* for them.

2.6 Semantics: Denotation and connotation

Chapter 1 mentions the usefulness of synonyms, antonyms, paraphrase and definition for the teaching of denotation. Example 24 provides some examples. There is often a fine line of distinction dividing synonymy, definition and paraphrase.

EXAMPLE 24

(a) *Definition*:

(i) Bungalow. T: And it means a home with only one floor.

(ii) Poster. T: A big, something colourful to put on the wall...

(iii) Partner. T: Your partner means the person that you are next to...

(b) *Synonymy*:

(i) Detached. T: It means alone.

(ii) Main. T: The main food, the usual food, is antelope.

(c) *Antonymy*:

Good Friday. S: What Good Friday?

      T: Good Friday...Christmas is when Jesus was born, when he was a baby, that is the day we celebrate for that. And then Good Friday is the day he died.

(d) *Paraphrase*:

(i) Interesting. T: Do you think Retford is interesting? Is it interesting? Is it em...can you find things to do there?

(ii) Move. T: Why did she move, why did she go away from Bolton?

An important point to keep in mind when providing definitions is that learners appear to require explanation of *both* description *and* function (Example 25):

EXAMPLE 25

(a) T: Keep her nice and warm... Fur coat yes...this is a fur coat: for the winter...made from er sometimes real animal skins but usually made by man...
Description: made from skins/by man.
Function: for the winter/keep warm.

(a) T: Utility. Yes this is a room where em...Mrs Smith does the washing...that's where the washing is done and the washing machine would be here and a drier perhaps...
Description: washing machine here/drier.
Function: where the washing is done.

(c) T: What do you call the special big shoes that come up to here for when it's snowing?
Description: big shoes/come up to here.
Function: for when it's snowing.

Problems of comprehension seem to arise if *only* description or *only* function is given, as in Example 26:

EXAMPLE 26

(a) T: Let's go...(shows picture)...skating shall we?
T: Skating, for dance?
Description: picture.
Function: missing, requested by student.

(b) T: Porch. It means em where you stand em sheltered waiting for the front door to be opened. You you come to the house, ring the bell, and you don't sta...in this house you don't have to stand in the rain if it's raining...
S: Like this second doors here?
Description: missing, requested by student.
Function where you stand sheltered waiting for door to be opened/in this house don't stand in rain.

Blum and Levenson[12] warn against unsuccessful paraphrase offered as explanation in class leading to misuse outside, if the teacher uses abnormal collocations which are taken to be normal. We can see that this is a danger with both paraphrases in 24(d). A similar danger pertains to definition and synonymy, as we can see from a look at 24(a)(iii) and (b)(ii). Examples in other contexts are needed for a full understanding of these terms.

Using an antonym may make meaning clearer. Words are only signs after all, and it is the *difference* between signs that defines them.

Moreover, we should not forget that no true antonyms or synonyms exist; they are merely so in the context in which they occur ('black' is not the antonym of 'white' when wine is the context). Spoken interaction may give rise to strange pragmatic antonyms such as accident/excellent (Example 27).

EXAMPLE 27

T: Excellent.
S: And like, em, words, er, eksident.
T: Accident. It sounds like accident, doesn't it? Excellent, accident. . . (writes)
S: Accident, excellent.
T: Accident, ooh dear, terrible! Excellent, very, very good.

Because of the importance of context to the notions of antonymy and synonymy, exercises which simply require a learner to produce one or the other without regard to context are of doubtful value. Spender,[13] at any rate, feels that non-gradable antonyms are the product of a patriarchal society which has taught us to think in binary terms like male/female, right/wrong: there is in fact a continuum rather than an opposition, so that any given male may display more or fewer feminine characteristics than another, or anybody may be 'a little bit wrong'. Certainly modern advances in medicine have led us to question even the non-gradability of alive/dead!

As well as knowing that, e.g. a 'shirt' is a garment worn above the waist, having a collar and fastening at the front with buttons (*de*notation), we need to know that it is worn by men only (*con*notation). The same garment worn by women is normally referred to as a 'blouse'. While women may in some circumstances use the term 'shirt', it is never acceptable for men to use 'blouse' when describing such a garment as worn by men. We need to familiarise to our learners the accepted connotations of new items of vocabulary, especially since many are highly culture specific. Example 28 gives instances from teachers and students:

EXAMPLE 28

(a) *W.C.*   S: But I see in er building they say 'toilet' no say . .
                T: Toilet, yes fine. Some people say W.C. That is a builder's word,
                    probably . . .
(b) *Aftershave*.   T: Some aftershave. That's perfume for men.
(c) *Can't stand*.   S: I can't stand it, this is 'it', for music or for man?
                T: That's right, it's for the music. You can use it of a person too.
                S: Can I say . . .
                T: I can't stand you.
                S: Ah, I can't stand him.
                T: Yes.

This aspect of word study has received much current attention because of its relevance to ideology. In the world of advertising, for example, among the adjectives which seem to help sell products today are 'clean', 'wholesome', 'natural'. In tourism, positive value is attached to items such as 'panoramic', 'picturesque', 'fresh', 'exotic', but also to others such as 'blue (sky and water)', 'medicinal (waters)', 'traditional (crafts, hospitality)' and 'old (buildings)', which in other contexts might have a neutral or even a negative bias. Notice the positive value assigned to 'teeming', 'huge', 'busy' 'familiar' and 'too narrow' in the following extract from a travel brochure.

> **You'll quickly
> discover that really there are two cities,
> the old and the new. Old Rome is a
> teeming maze of alleys, ancient palaces
> and huge buildings - try the Colosseum
> for size! Then there is the new Rome
> which is busy, animated and
> cosmopolitan with elegant shops
> displaying familiar designer labels,
> abundant restaurants and evening
> entertainments. Rome is very much a
> place to explore on foot with many
> delightful sights hidden in streets too
> narrow for vehicles to pass.**

Feminist writers are particularly concerned with semantics in so far as it concerns the concept of 'gender'. Many languages have 'grammatical gender' where, e.g., masculine/feminine/neuter is merely a three-way classification reflecting the fact that their nouns behave differently when it comes to agreement of adjectives, choice of article, replacement by pronoun. The classification does not reflect a distinction of word meaning into male, female and inanimate. English does not have 'grammatical' but rather 'natural' gender. Feminists have pointed out that English gender is 'natural' only if you are a man, that in fact there *is* a connection between grammatical gender and sex. That the masculine is the unmarked, or neutral, term is not simply a feature of grammar: as Example 29 shows, words which are normally thought of as capable of *either* a masculine *or* a feminine interpretation are in fact *only* masculine:

EXAMPLE 29[14]

'Fourteen *survivors*, three of them women . . .'
'*People* are much more likely to be influenced by their wives than by opinion polls.'
'When the first *ancestor* of the human race descended from the trees, she had not yet developed the mighty brain that was to distinguish her so sharply from other species.'
'*Man* suffers backaches, ruptures easily and has difficulty giving birth.'

Feminist research indicates that children think of 'man' as male in sentences such as 'man needs food', that science students think male when discussing the evolution of 'man', but that females do not think of *themselves* when using generic 'he' or 'man'. Consequently females use these terms less frequently and only then based on standards of grammatical correctness. Sexism in vocabulary study is a vast area of current concern, as yet largely ignored by textbook writers, with the welcome exception of Viney (Example 30).

EXAMPLE 30[15]

Sexism in words

'Sexist'	Neutral
chairman/woman	chairperson
salesman/woman	salesperson
air hostess	flight attendant
housewife	homemaker
actor/actress	actor
Mrs/Miss	Ms
he ...	he or she/they

Exercise 3

Make a table with columns labelled 'male', 'female' or 'neutral'. Put these words into the columns depending on whether you think they apply to one more than another. Discuss your choice with a partner.

aggressive	ambitious	sympathetic
shy	confident	quiet
beautiful	handsome	strong
competitive	caring	gentle
kind	rude	polite
nagging	gossip	discussion
chat	talk	complaining
efficient	argue	row
cry	weep	brave
brutal		

RIGHT, WHO'S GOING TO BE MOTHER AND POUR THE TEA?

CHAIRPERSON

2.7 Polysemy and the relationship of sound to spelling

We have seen (Chapter 1.5) how the acoustic element (the way a word sounds) is of great importance at lower levels of proficiency, so teachers of elementary learners should be careful to teach pronunciation of new lexical items, not just in isolation but contrastively, as in Example 31:

EXAMPLE 31

T: What does *supper* mean?
S: Super is very good, super.
T: Ah that's 'super', s..u..p..e..r.
S: Yes.
T: One 'p'. This is double 'p', *supper*.
S: Double 'p'.
T: *Supper*, what's *supper*?
S: Usually eating.
T: Yes it's a meal you have in the evening.

We should guard against encouraging learners to make out of context guesses. In Example 32, the teacher assumes that the learners will refer to their written text for clues, but omits to show them strategies for doing so, thus unwittingly encouraging them to guess wildly:

EXAMPLE 32

T: (looking at given text) Do you know what *token* means? What's a record *token*?
S: Speaking, like speaking (confusion with 'talking')
S: Like er record er something er electric or . . .
S: Token (talking) some cassette recording I think.

Students can be trained to work out meanings in *written* English by looking at large chunks of discourse. Left to their own devices, they also work hard to match phonology and syntax in order to interpret meanings in *spoken* discourse, as Example 33 shows:

EXAMPLE 33

(Phonetic script is used to show S's strategies more clearly.)
S: If you give me £5 ɑl bɑɪə ʃʊz
T: A pair of shoes
S: ɑ pɛə ə ʃʊz
T: Can you say it again?
S: ɑ pɛə ə ʃʊz
T: I'll buy . . .
S: ə pɑɪ ə ʃʊz
T: A pair of shoes.
S: I'll buy a pair of shoes.

2.8 Mother tongue

In their attempts to communicate, learners may substitute an L1 item for its L2 equivalent, alter an L1 term to fit the morphology or pronunciation of the L2, or guess word meaning by using a false cognate, i.e. a similar sounding word in the mother tongue. In monolingual groups, translation is a very important method of familiarisation among students, and there seem to be two ways of using it. Firstly, it can be a simple preface or reinforcement to learning, normally a direct L1 equivalent of one or two words in length. Secondly, it can be a strategy for clarifying meaning, and therefore a longer utterance or even a conversation between learners. Example 34 gives illustrations of the first type, (a) being the use of L1 as a preface to word search, (b) being the use of L1 as consolidation of learning, and (c) being the use of L1 both as preface *and* consolidation:

EXAMPLE 34

(a) S: Take his er...(L1 for *blood*) mm...er...(mimes)...*blood*.
(b) T: You're under *cover*.
     S: Oh yes.
     S: (L1 for *cover*)
     S: Yes cover (L1 for cover)
(c) T: Let's go to the...where do you find animals?
     S: (L1 for *zoo*)
     S: In er...*zoo*.
     S: *Zoo*.
     T: Yes, let's go to the *zoo*.
     S: (L1 for *zoo*)

When using L1 as a strategy for clarifying meaning, one student may make a quick familiarisation to another without teacher intervention, or there may be a general discussion signalling that further teacher-directed clarification is needed.

Thus, even if we do not speak the L1 of our learners, we can be sensitive to the following cues:

1. A simple one-word utterance in the L1 may be taken as a good sign that meaning is understood.
2. Prolonged discussion in the L1 may signal one student's difficulty in comprehension, which is being explained by another. Intervention may be required by the teacher to clarify matters.[16]

2.9 Tasks

Group tasks

1. Choose a short text of a level suitable for your students. Pick out three vocabulary items from it that you think your students will not know, and discuss ways of *pre-familiarising* these three items, using (a) non-verbal, (b) written and (c) oral/aural stimulus.
2. Discuss the function of 'giving advice' and decide on which ways of doing this you would teach to give a spread of formal and informal language.
3. Choose three vocabulary items and discuss how you could use (a) definition, (b) synonymy and (c) antonymy to make the meaning clear to your class.
4. Discuss the connotations of these words with regard to masculine/feminine, positive/negative parameters: 'petty', 'physique', 'picturesque', 'piercing', 'pigheaded', 'plucky'.

Self-assessed tasks

1. For each extract below, say which aspect of 'knowledge of a word' is being familiarised:

    (a) T: What is it? (writes slowly on board)
        S. Feth...
        T: Feth (finishes writing word)
        S: fɛðiər
        T: Feather.
        S: Feather.

    (b) S: Could you explain the difference between school and college?
        T: A college is usually for students over sixteen.

    (c) T: If you were my friend and I was disagreeing with you I might say, 'Oh come on' or 'You've got to be joking', but what would I say if you were my boss and I disagreed with you?
        S: 'I'm afraid I can't agree.'

    (d) T: This man is a careful driver, so he drives...
        S: Carefully.
        T: And this woman has fluent German, so she speaks...
        S: She speaks German fluently.

    (e) T: I know that you have the word 'sensible' in your language, but in English it doesn't mean the same thing.

2. For each of the following extracts, say whether it demonstrates pre- or post-familiarisation, and say which stimulus it uses:

    (a) S: *Interesting* (reading from text)
        T: Do you think Retford is *interesting*?
        S: Retford.
        T: Is it *interesting*? Is is em...can you find things to do there?
        S: No.
        T: Not very many. Retford isn't very *interesting*.
        S: *Interesting*.
        T: Sheffield is more *interesting*. It has discos, theatres, cinemas, big shops...
        S: Yeah, *interesting*.

    (b) T: Those (shows pictures) What are those called?
        S: Skri?
        T: *Skis*.
        S: *Skis*.

    (c) T: What colour is a camel?
        S: Brown, no like er...
        S_2: Like chocolate.
        S_3: White orange.
        T: *Beige*.
        SS: *Beige*.

    (d) T: Do you find it *exciting*?
        S: What *exciting*, is er interesting?
        T: It's more than interesting.
        S: *Exciting*.
        T: ...so that you're shouting, 'Get a goal, get a goal, watch out!' and, you know, there's more than just interest.
        S: *Exciting* (L1 for 'exciting')

Notes and references

1. I first met the terms 'pre-familiarisation' and 'post-familiarisation' in a thesis by Michael Burke, presented in part fulfilment of the degree of MA in Applied English Linguistics, University of Birmingham.
2. R. Carter, 'Is there a core vocabulary? Some implications for language teaching', *Applied Linguistics* 1987 **8(2)**: 178–93.
3. H. Widdowson, *Learning Purpose and Language Use*, Oxford University Press, 1983, p. 93.
4. Example 15 is from P. Harvey and C. Walker, *Way Ahead* (3), Penguin, 1986.
5. Example 17a is from P. Hanks, 'How common is common?', Introduction to *Collins Cobuild Dictionary Diary*, 1989.

6. Example 17b concordances from the Birmingham Collection of English Text (Collins Cobuild).
7. D. Willis, 'A lexical approach to syllabus design', *EFL Gazette* August 1988: 10–11.
8. D. Willis and J. Willis, *The Cobuild English Course, op. cit.*
9. J. Sinclair, 'Naturalness in language', *English Language Research Journal* 1988, ns., vol. II: 203–10.
10. R. Hindmarsh, *The Cambridge English Lexicon*, Cambridge University Press, 1980.
11. G. Fox, 'Examples that make you think', paper given at IATEFL Conference, 1986.
12. S. Blum and E.A. Levenson, 'Universals of lexical simplification', *Language Learning* 1978, **28(2)**: 399–415.
13. D. Spender, *Man Made Language*, Routledge & Kegan Paul, 1980, p. 189.
14. D. Cameron, *Feminism and Linguistic Theory*, Macmillan, 1985, p. 69; and D. Spender *op. cit.*, p. 152.
15. Example 30 is from P. Viney, *Streamline English Directions*, Oxford University Press, 1985.
16. For more about the use of L1 as a strategy, see L. Taylor, 'Vocabulary in interaction' (see ch. 3, Notes and References).

Chapter 3

Repetition and Interaction

3.1 How can I tell if my explanation has been understood?

The best evidence of understanding comes from feedback from students. We can best obtain feedback by eliciting a *response*, and three economical ways of doing this are as follows:

1. Posing a direct question, e.g. 'Do you think Retford is *interesting*?' . . .(pause)
2. Using a tag, e.g. 'Football is *exciting*, don't you think so? It's exciting to watch and exciting to play isn't it? . . .(pause)
3. Rising intonation, e.g. 'Her *parents*, her mother and father?' . . .(pause)

By using these simple means of eliciting a quick 'yes' or 'no', teachers can gain some idea of how well the new item has been understood. There is one word of warning, however: both teachers and learners have a low tolerance of silence in the classroom. Teachers avoid silence by rephrasing their question, as in Example 35:

EXAMPLE 35

> T: Are you going to miss your dinner? (pause) Are you going to miss a meal? (pause) Not go to a meal? (pause)

However, if a teacher's pause is uncomfortably long, a student may feel obliged to fill the gap even though he does not fully understand, as in Example 36:

EXAMPLE 36

> T: In this house you don't have to stand in the rain (pause) If it's raining (pause)
> S: Mmm.
> T: No. You don't see.

Another pitfall to avoid is that of asking 'Do you understand?' . . .(pause), to which there will always be a favourable reply!

We have to check learning by more specific means, such as asking for pronunciation, spelling or a simple definition.

3.2   How can I ensure that my students will be able to use the vocabulary I have taught them?

Learners remember best those items which have recurred many times, and especially those which they have uttered themselves.[1] The role of repetition cannot be underestimated, which is one of the reasons why cyclical syllabuses are now so popular.[2] Choral or at least teacher-directed repetition does aid recall, and individual student repetition of an item, especially if it can be done with humour, is most effective (Example 37):

EXAMPLE 37

S:	What's a *meal*?
T:	A *meal*, to eat.
S:	Yeah. To eat. He like...
S:	Go to the *meal*, I like go.
S:	A *meal*.
T:	A *meal*, yes.
S:	*Greedy*.
T:	(Go out for a *meal*)...Mr *Greedy*.
S:	All *greedy* yeah, ha ha (L1 equivalent)
S:	He all the times he want...
T:	I have a book at home called 'Mr *Greedy*'.
All:	(laughter)

...(later same lesson)...

S:	Let's have a party.
S:	*Greedy*.

One *caveat* concerning the use of choral repetition: students may be ill at ease if asked to repeat an item whose 'sense' has not been familiarised first (Example 38):

EXAMPLE 38

T:	Say it.
S:	*Utility*?
T:	Yes, very good, can you say that?
S:	*Utility*.
T:	*Utility*.
S:	Same toilet?
T:	I can explain it in a moment, you say it first.

Some teachers may not feel confident at directing choral repetition, since it does demand something of a bandleader's skill! A less overt way of effecting repetition is to use a questioning technique rather than simply to model the item. In Examples 39 and 40, the teacher uses a chain of choice questions:

EXAMPLE 39

T: We call it *domestic*, but an eagle?
S: Not *domestic*.
T: ...is not *domestic*.
S: *Domestic*.
T: What about a dog, is a dog wild or *domestic* usually in England?
S: *Domestic*.
T: And a cat?
S: *Domestic*.
T: A sheep?

EXAMPLE 40

(Teacher uses series of pictures.)
T: Is he excited, or *bored*?
S: *Bored*.
T: And this woman here?
S: *Bored*.
T: What about the other man, what do you think about him?
S: Very *bored*.

A further way of achieving a number of repetitions is for the *teacher* to repeat the item, but to require the learners to respond appropriately (Example 41):

EXAMPLE 41

T: What *date* is it today? It's the 13th, yes.
S: But *day*?
T: *Day*. Monday, Tuesday, Wednesday...
S: Ah.
T: What *date* is it tomorrow?
S: It's 14th November.
T: 14th November tomorrow, isn't it? What *day* is it today?
S: It's Tuesday.
S: Aha.

3.3   How can I improve the effectiveness of my initial vocabulary teaching?

The short answer to this question is 'Be sensitive to likely difficulties. If possible try to predict them and be ready with explanations.' In particular we should be sensitive to problems of L1 transfer. However, since this type of interference will vary greatly according to the linguistic background of our learners, it is not possible to generalise here. Other dangers of a universal nature are illustrated below.

3.3.1   Danger 1: Encouraging under- or over-generalisation

In Example 42, it is clear from the negotiation that the use of a magazine picture of a stage has posed two problems for the students: (a) the concept of audience and participators – are we talking about the actors on stage, or about the audience? and (b) how narrow is the definition of 'theatre'; does it include opera *and* plays *and* ballet, or just opera (as the student surmises)? The stimulus in this case is ambiguous, and it would have been preferable to use another depicting a theatre building or perhaps to use a video excerpt:

EXAMPLE 42

T: What shall we do? (shows picture of theatre stage with actors)
S: Dancing, singing, singing.
T: Ah we're not going to dance we're going to watch...
S: Watch.
T: ...and we're going to see this. Where...what is the place where you go to listen to music or watch actors?
S: Cincema cinema.
T: But this is live, people on the stage acting...it's a...
S: (L1 for *theatre*)
T: *Theatre*.
S: *Theatre theatre* is er for the singing?

3.3.2   Danger 2: Omitting to teach by contrasts

If, for example, we have to teach the item 'ground floor', we can predict at least two problems: the confusion of 'ground' with 'earth' and perhaps with 'underground', and the polysemy of 'floor' which means both 'ground' and 'storey'. It is therefore sensible to teach by contrast with 'first floor', 'basement', 'second floor'. In the following, we can notice the danger associated with the use of 'or', which can be confusing to students because of its meaning as 'alternative to' rather than 'equal to': 'This is upstairs or this is first floor or upstairs.'

3.3.3 Danger 3: Choosing an inappropriate stimulus

We noted this point in our discussion of Danger 1, where the single still picture of actors on stage was not adequate as an eliminating context. There are occasions where it may be preferable simply to rely on an oral/aural stimulus alone. In Example 43 the pictures do not help make meaning clear, but throw attention away from the item being taught, i.e. *exciting*, on to the activities depicted in the visuals:

EXAMPLE 43

> T: What are they doing? (shows picture of sailing)
> S: Sailing.
> T: Sailing. Is sailing *exciting*?
> S: Yes.
> T: It's *exciting*...yes. Do you ever watch em this kind of sport? (shows picture of horse racing)
> S: Horses, sports, horse race...
> T: Horse racing...do you find it *exciting*?

3.3.4 Danger 4: Asking stupid questions

Purely mechanical learning comes more naturally to children than to adults. As we can see from Example 1, where the mother asks 'What colour's that?', a question to which she already knows the answer, they do not worry about 'unnatural' language of this type. Adults, however, may feel that they are being patronised if we ask such a question. We can achieve the same result by other means. For example, if we wish to teach a colour adjective, e.g. 'beige', instead of pointing to an object and asking 'What colour is this?' (when everybody can see what colour it is anyway), we can say 'Do you like the colour *beige*?' In this way we encourage learners to respond with '*Beige*? What's beige?', to which we can respond '*Beige*. This is *beige*' (pointing to the object).

3.3.5 Danger 5: Making explanations less than explicit

In naturally occurring conversation, as we have seen from Example 2, familiarisations tend to be glossed over quickly, so that they are not really perceived as such at all. In the formal teaching of vocabulary we need to make sure that our familiarisations are clearly perceived as explanations, not additions. Example 44 shows two explanations which are unsuccessful:

EXAMPLE 44

(a) *Interested*:
T: He is *interested*, he's looking at it very carefully. He doesn't notice anybody else.

(b) *Ugly*:
T: Why he's *ugly*, he doesn't look nice uh? No.
S: Sad.
T: Now the thing is . . .

                              — — —

S: What does *ugly* mean please?

It is not clear that 'he doesn't look nice' is meant as a paraphrase of *ugly*, nor that 'he's looking at it very carefully' and 'he doesn't notice anyone' are meant as paraphrases of '*he* is *interested*'. Moreover the paraphrases themselves are most misleading, since one may look nice while still being *ugly*, and one may look carefully while not being *interested*. A further point to notice is that the teacher does not comment on his student's volunteered synonym, *sad* (Example 44(b)), thus failing to provide confirmation or disconfirmation of the meaning hypothesis.

In order to avoid such ambiguity we need to make our explanation explicit, for example in one of the following ways:

1. Using a phrase such as 'That means . . .'.
2. Using a slow, clearly enunciated delivery for the item being taught.
3. Making the item salient by saying it more loudly or at higher pitch.
4. Eliciting a number of repetitions of the item.
5. Using more than one synonym, paraphrase or example in context.
6. Attending to both semantic and acoustic parameters of the item, i.e. both meaning and sound.

3.3.6 Danger 6: Asking learners to concentrate simultaneously on both meaning and form

It is better to teach the *meaning* of an item first, i.e. its semantic aspect, and then its *form*, i.e. aspects of pronunciation, spelling, morphology, syntax. In this way we can avoid overloading our learners' capacities. For example, in spoken interaction involving vocabulary teaching, we might have on the one hand negotiation for meaning, which focuses on content, and on the other hand choral repetition, which emphasises form.

The more ways we can use to familiarise vocabulary, the better chance we have of making the meaning understood, so it is a good idea to teach several of the seven aspects of 'knowledge of a word' together, using a combination of stimuli. It is also beneficial for learners, especially adults, to write down items needed for active use. The importance of context can be emphasised by introducing the new item in several sentences, tying them into the overall discourse. Where possible we should also relate new meanings to our learners' own experience.

3.4 Tasks

Group tasks

1. Choose three vocabulary items and discuss how you could achieve enough student repetition of the new items *without* using choral repetition, i.e. either using choice questions with student repetition, or using questioning technique with teacher repetition.

2. Study this example and discuss ways in which the teacher could have avoided the confusion which leads to prolonged discussion in L1:

   T: This we call a *bungalow*, only one floor, all right?
   S_1: *Bungalow.*
   T: Yes.
   S_1: *Bungalow* only one floor, no rooms inside.
   S_2: Yeh, there is room inside, like flat, no?
   T: Yes. It means a home with only one floor, no upstairs.
   S_2: All the bedroom down.
   T: All the bedrooms everything downstairs OK?
   S_2: Store, or what that?
   S_3: *Bungalow*, house.
   S_1: *Bungalow*, teacher, bungalow is building with er bricks, or with plywood?
   T: Ah, doesn't matter...brick, breeze block, corrugated iron, tin, it is the one, only one floor that makes it a *bungalow*.
   S_2: *Bungalow.*
   All: (students: discussion in L1, quite prolonged)
   S_2: Like er market, one floor same market?
   S_3: Same the store?
   S_2: Here flat where I stay that is a *bungalow*? My bedroom where I stay now is...
   T: Oh no no because...
   S_2 There's one floor.

3. Choose two of the following lexical items and discuss ways of teaching form and meaning, with reference to your own learners:

actually	sympathetic	sensitive	funny
borrow	refuse	too	machine
chips	licence	control	

Self-assessed tasks

1. Look at the three ways given at the beginning of this chapter of eliciting feedback
    from students to show whether they have understood a new vocabulary item. Now
    say which of these three ways is being used in each of the following extracts:

    (a) T: What is a cobra covered in? Has it got feathers?
         S: No.

    (b) S: She er heard some sound, some sound for the one boy, one man is er like
             open the cupboard and open the things there...
         T: Oh, some *burglars* were in her house?
         S: Yes, and she heard.

    (c) S: They got the diver men coming inside the water and take the camera and
             the light...
         T: Oh, the *frogmen* went down, did they?
         S. Yes, the *frogmen*, yes.

2. Look at Section 3.3.5 of this chapter (Danger 5), which gives six ways of making
    explanations explicit. Say which of these ways is/are being used in each of the following
    familiarisations of new vocabulary items:

    (a) (J. and F. are students; T. is teacher.)
         J: *Still* in London.
         F: *Still* there.
         T: But I am now in Retford yes.
         F: But the word *still*.
         T: Yes.
         F: ...er another *still*.
         T: Another meaning yes.
         F: The catch anything.
         T: *Still*.
         F: *Still* yes.
         T: Stand *still*.
         F: And the thief is *still*.
         T: Yes...oh.
         F: The thief is *still*.
         T: Steal, that's *steal*, different spelling, yes *steal, steal*.
         All: *Steal*.
         T: But this is *still*. I (writes) *still* live in Retford. And another meaning...
         F: *Still* not.
         T: Stand *still*. Yes, same spelling, stand *still, still* but this different.
         F: And *steal*.
         T: *Steal*.

    S: I can say next weekend.
    T: Mm.
    S: My friend is going London. . .
    T   Yes.
    F: I'm *still* here.

(b) (J. and A. are students; T. is teacher.)
    T: Can you tell me what *detached* means? (points to picture)
    J: What *detached* mean?
    T: *Detached* yes.
    J: What is what.
    T: It means (ask me!). . .it means alone, not joined together.
    J: Siprate.
    T: Now they are together. . .*detached*, together (mime)
    J: Siprait no?
    T: Separate. Separate, absolutely, separate?
    J , A : Separate.

(c) (J. and F. students, T is teacher.)
    T: What's this?
    J: Person.
    A: Percent huh?
    T: And what's this?
    J: Prison.
    F: Present.
    T: Now they're not the same. *Per cent, present.*
    All: *Per cent, present.*
    T: Yes now this is 'z' OK? That's 's' and this is 'z'. . .

Notes and references

1   This point is elaborated in L. Taylor, 'Vocabulary in interaction', unpublished project submitted for the degree of MA in Applied English Linguistics, University of Birmingham, 1986, and also in M. McKeown, I. Beck, R. Omanson and M. Pople, 'Some effects of the nature and the frequency of vocabulary instruction on the knowledge and use of words', *Reading Research Quarterly* Fall 1985, **XX/5**.

2.   Such syllabuses build into a course a systematic recycling and reviewing of language already taught in previous units. For example, the simple past tense might be introduced initially in the context of relating a sequence of events on the theme of 'What I did yesterday' and recycled for a later unit in the context of a recipe and describing a process — 'How I made this dish'.

Chapter 4

Exercises for Consolidation

4.1 Now that I've taught the vocabulary item, what further practice can I provide?

Systematic word study is becoming increasingly integrated into general English language courses, right from beginner level. Many current textbooks include imaginative vocabulary exercises which we can adapt for our own teaching needs.

Let's look at some of these exercises and relate them to our seven categories of 'knowledge of a word'.

4.1.1 Frequency

We can consult word lists[1] in order to ascertain the level of frequency of items we have taught. Graded readers use such lists to limit the basic vocabulary, so that learners have a familiar context from which to infer the meaning of the unfamiliar word. Pictures and diagrams also help to provide such a context.[2] In Example 45a words which are likely to be unfamiliar to students are replaced by nonsense words, thus simulating how the text would look to a foreign learner.

EXAMPLE 45a[3]

How easy do you think it is to guess the meanings of words from clues in the picture?

Example 3 ... interdependence of text and illustrations ...

It is the 26th July. Mr and Mrs Davies and Catherine are in the car. They are stribbing to the flamp.

"Catherine, have you got your giltip and your valmet?" Mr Davies says.

"Yes, Dad," Catherine says. "You've asked me that ten grums. Here's my giltip and here's my valmet."

It can be motivating for students to give *them* the initiative in saying which words they want to learn. Some words may have high frequency for particular students because of their career or sphere of interest — as in Example 45b:

EXAMPLE 45b[4]

> ' "Prevent" is very useful — it must be because I already know it.'
> ' "Aware" — I didn't know this word but it looks useful.'
> ' "Gaol/Jail" — I know the word "prison", so "gaol" isn't necessary.'
> (We pointed out that 'gaol' might be useful receptively for this level of student as it appears frequently in newspaper texts.)
> ' "Beam" — it's a technological word so it may become more important in the future; that's why I chose to learn it.'
> (We pointed out that for a banker with no specific interest in technology, this item probably wasn't very useful.)
> ' "Launch" — this word will be useful because I work in marketing.'
> 'I want to learn them all. I think they're all useful.'
> (We suggested to this student that her approach might interfere with the learning of more useful items.)
> ' "Moor" — I'm very interested in boats so this word will be useful.'
> Student: 'Moor' — is this word only used for boats?
> Teacher: Yes.
> Student: In that case I don't want to learn it.
>
> This type of activity can be very revealing for the teacher as a means of understanding his students' needs and attitudes towards learning.

The concept of frequency is rather an abstract one however. We can use frequency counts to show us which items to use at a given level of language competence, but for the purposes of written exercises, frequency is inextricably tied to the sister concept of register when it comes to usage. The most successful way to explore the two concepts is the contrastive one, for example informal/formal, or friendly/belligerent, where context of situation can be taken into account.

4.1.2 Register

The relationship between register and frequency is vividly demonstrated in this simple comparison of article titles (Example 46). The left-hand column shows the original titles of articles appearing in scientific and technical journals, whilst the right-hand column shows the corresponding title of popularised versions appearing in the *New Scientist*.

EXAMPLE 46[5]

Journal title	Newspaper title
Parental Investment and Sex Differences in Juvenile Mortality in Birds and Mammals	**Biologists ponder plight of vulnerable male**
Do Frogs Communicate with Seismic Signals?	**How a frog means more by a croak**
The Possible Link Between Net Surface Heating and 'El Nino'	**Iguanas in peril from ocean changes**

Teachers may like to try a similar comparison by taking articles either from newspapers of general interest or from those dealing with their learners' specialities.

Example 47 shows another type of exercise dealing with scientific and technical register:

EXAMPLE 47[6]

Which of the following sentences would you be most likely to find in a technical or specialised context?
(a) She has a big nose.
(b) He studied the proboscis of the insect.
(c) This water is salty.
(d) Water in which salt has been dissolved is called a saline solution.
(e) The eyeballs are covered with a thin membrane.
(f) He has a sore knee.

Kennedy and Bolitho[7] speak of the difficulty learners meet when words commonly occurring in 'general' English take on a specialised meaning within a scientific or technical context, e.g. *cycle, conductor, resistance*, so teachers of ESP may find the above exercise useful.

Examples 48a–c show three ways of treating the formal/informal opposition:

EXAMPLE 48a[8]

Each of these sentences contains a mixture of formal and informal English. Rewrite them so that they sound like casual informal speech throughout:
(i)   I was so fatigued as to be obliged to retire at the same time as the kids.
(ii) The little boy sought an audience with his Mum in order to ask her what steps she had taken with regard to all his football clobber.
(iii) There is a high probability that Dad would do his nut should he learn of this catastrophe.

EXAMPLE 48b[8]

All of the following sentences are written in formal English. Write down the word in each sentence which shows that the sentence is formal:
(i)   He took his habitual glass of wine before going to bed.
(ii) The fact is not germane to the present argument.
(iii) The pupil has made a laudable attempt to help his less fortunate classmates with their work.
(iv) These curtains will impart an air of luxury to your bedroom.

EXAMPLE 48c[8]

Write out the following sentences and underline the slang phrase contained in each of them:
(i)   He got the boot for always being late.
(ii) When the firm was unable to pay higher wages the employees put the boot in and went on strike although they knew it would bankrupt the firm.
(iii) He left his job because he was cheesed off.

4.1.3 *Collocation*

Any given lexical item keeps company with either of the following:

1. Words which have a syntagmatic relationship with it (i.e. which can stand next to it in a sentence).
2. Words which form a set of related content items, occurring more distantly in the sentence, even occurring across the sentence boundary (see example of 'overtake' in section 1.2).

Examples 49a and 49b give exercises to practise the first relationship.

EXAMPLE 49a[9]

C   Exercises

CI Match the words on the left side with those on the right side as in the example.

1 a loaf of	☐	flour
2 five	☐	sugar
3 two packets of	☐	flowers
4 a role of	☐	cigarettes
5 a bottle of	☐ *1*	bread
6 a bag of	☐	kitchen paper
7 twenty	☐	books
8 a bunch of	☐	apples
9 a kilo of	☐	medicine
10 a pound of	☐	tea

EXAMPLE 49b[9]

> As pretty as a picture.

We often use these idioms to describe people.

Can you match them up?

As pretty as   an ox
As obstinate as   gold
As white as   a picture
As strong as   a mouse
As good as   a sheet
As quiet as   a mule

We can also let students 'brainstorm' their own 'connections' for a given word, to produce a 'word network' like this one for *Friend*:

EXAMPLE 50[10]

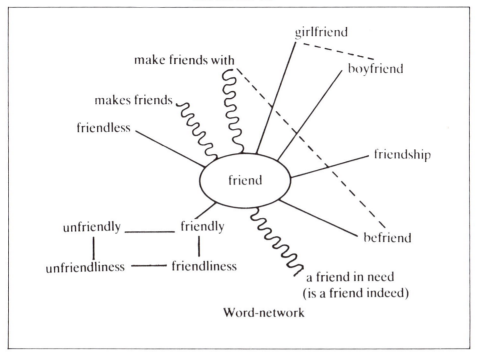

Word-network

Idioms are a great source of difficulty for foreign learners. One of the problems here is the fact that they haved fixed collocations. For example 'spic' is a word which does not exist outside the expression 'spic and span'. Michael Wallace gives this list of how strange an idiom would sound if the collocations were broadened:

They have let several cats out of bags.
He goes about licking people's sandals.
Yesterday it rained dogs and cats.
The teacup has just had a storm.

Another problem with idioms is that their meaning cannot be inferred from the literal meaning of the words within the expression. Wallace advocates teaching idioms (and phrasal verbs too) just as unusually long words, i.e. as individual lexical items, like any simple word. He also thinks they are best taught in context. Two exercises for practising idioms are given in Examples 51a and 51b.

EXAMPLE 51a[11]

Match each verbal idiom in capitals with one of the meanings below, and check
your results with the Dictionary:
(i)   It can't be true! You're PULLing my LEG.
(ii) We all told him he couldn't have seen a mermaid, but he stuck (STICK) to his
      GUNS.
(iii) I know the shop's closed on Sunday by law, but couldn't you just STRETCH
      A POINT and sell me some bread?
(iv) Whenever we play tennis he always BEATs me HOLLOW.
to make fun of a person in a playful way
to continue to fight or argue in spite of attacks
to defeat someone completely
to allow a little freedom from a rule, especially on a special occasion

EXAMPLE 51b[11]

Below is a list of idioms, followed by seven sentences in which expressions equivalent
in meaning to the idioms are italicised. Match each idiom to its explanatory sentence:

blue-blooded   splitting hairs   wide of the mark

(i)   Your assessment of the situation is *completely wrong and nowhere near the truth.*
(ii) He claimed special social privileges on the grounds that he was *of noble descent.*
(iii) We are wasting the committee's time by *arguing too much over unimportant
      details.*

Example 52 shows the second type relationship of collocations:

EXAMPLE 52a[12]

a   *Find the odd one out*. Which word does not belong to the group? Why?
b   *Give each group in the box a name.*

Pop groups	S _____	C _____	S _____	H _____
The Police	Football	Jeans	Table tennis	Collecting autographs
Markethill	Swimming	Sweatshirt	Basketball	Listening to music
Madness	Canoeing	Trousers	Rollerskating	Singing
Bucks Fizz	Sweaters	Blouse	Athletics	Homework
Polecats	Sailing	Shoes	Stamp collecting	Acting
Dollar	Gymnastics	Coat	Ice-skating	Photography
		Dancing		Computers
				Animals
				Playing the guitar

Students can be encouraged to form their own lexical sets as a pre-text activity, as in this one:

EXAMPLE 52b[12]

Predicting Words

Level: Intermediate−advanced

Time: 30−45 mins

Preparation

Choose a text with a fairly narrow and predictable set of vocabulary, by virtue of its content and/or style. Examples of suitable texts might be:

(i)   Advertisements.

(ii) New items dealing with a well-known or repeated theme (e.g. SALT talks, earthquake stories, election accounts).

(iii) Fairy stories and folk tales known to the students (e.g. Cinderella, Washington and the cherry tree, Nasreddin stories − depending on the students' backgrounds).

(iv) Instructions from grocery packets, household appliances, etc.

In class

(i)   Tell the students that later in in the lesson they will be reading a text/listening to a tape/hearing a story. Give them a very approximate idea of what the text will be about.

(ii) Then ask the students, in pairs, to predict the vocabulary that is in the advertisement. Tell them to produce a list of 8−12 items. Allow them to use dictionaries and to ask each other for help. Give assistance where asked for.

(iii) Ask the students, in groups of 8−12, to explain their lists to one another

(iv) Give out the text for comparison and discussion.

4.1.4 *Morphology*

The study of word formation includes the meaning of prefixes and suffixes. It also includes the identification of word classes. Many items of specialised vocabulary are made up of a root plus suffix or a prefix deriving from Greek or Latin, such as mono-, neo-, hyper-. Suffixes give clues to the grammatical function of a word, and there are many prefixes which transform an item into its opposite meaning, such as un-, dis-, non-. Here are four exercises which practise these relationships (Examples 53a−d):

EXAMPLE 53a[13]

The words in the columns below are taken from the text:
Verbs on the left, nouns on the right. For each verb supply an abstract noun with
the same root and for each noun a verb with the same root.

Verbs	*Nouns*
produce	production
_____	acceleration
_____	invention
_____	starvation
abolish	_____
create	_____

EXAMPLE 53b[13]

The following adjectives are taken from the two texts. Note their endings. Next to
each one write another adjective with a similar ending.

essent*ial*	crucial
elabor*ate*	_____
bas*ic*	_____
arbitr*ary*	_____
import*ant*	_____

EXAMPLE 53c[13]

Draw up a table on a separate sheet of paper. Divide it into columns, labelled as
follows:

_____ic/ _____ous/ _____able/ _____ive/ _____al/ _____ish/ _____ful/
_____less/ _____ent/ _____y/ _____ed/ _____abt

Put the words from the chart opposite in the columns.

The Rat	The Ox	The Tiger	The Rabbit	The Dragon	The Snake
aggressive	hard-working	smiling	cautious	showy	wise
energetic	lonely	magnetic	clever	artistic	sympathetic
jolly	leaders	lucky	hospitable	enthusiastic	lucky
charming	strong	strong	sociable	lucky	sophisticated
sociable	proud	honourable	friendly	healthy	calm
humorous	reserved	leaders	sensitive	generous	decisive
generous	methodical	liberal-minded	ambitious	sentimental	attractive
intellectual	original	courageous	careful	successful	philosophical
sentimental	eloquent	generous		independent	elegant
honest	patient	passionate			compassionate
persistent	silent				
greedy	rigid	vain	private	demanding	lazy
small-minded	bad losers	rash	timid	irritable	possessive
power-hungry	authoritarian	disobedient	thin-skinned	loud-mouthed	tight-fisted
destructive	conventional	undisciplined	old-fashioned	stubborn	bad losers
suspicious	jealous	argumentative	hypochondriac	discontented	changeable
tiresome	stubborn	rebellious	squeamish	wilful	vengeful
gamblers	slow				extravagant
Nixon	Chaplin	Elizabeth II	Einstein	John Lennon	J.F. Kennedy
Brando	Hitler	De Gaulle	Bob Hope	Ringo Starr	Jackie Kennedy
Shakespeare	Napoleon	Ayatollah Khomeini	Confucius	Al Pacino	Howard Hughes
Mozart	Walt Disney	Beethoven	Sinatra	Abraham Lincoln	Bob Dylan
Tolstoy	Mrs Thatcher	Marilyn Monroe		Freud	Mao Tse Tung
	Nehru			Charles Darwin	Gandhi

The Horse	The Goat	The Monkey	The Rooster	The Dog	The Pig
gifted	gentle	merry	proud	faithful	scrupulous
athletic	artistic	enthusiastic	enthusiastic	loyal	loyal
charming	peace-loving	witty	stylish	noble	sincere
quick-witted	sweet-natured	good in business	popular	modest	honest
hard-working	lovable	clever	lively	devoted	loving
entertaining	creative	fascinating	amusing	prosperous	sociable
powerful	inventive	passionate	generous	courageous	sensitive
skilful	amorous	youthful	adventurous	respectable	sensual
cheerful	tasteful	very intelligent	industrious	selfless	truthful
eloquent	intelligent	inventive	conservative	dutiful	peaceful
independent			courageous	intelligent	intelligent
weak	insecure	vain	pompous	introverted	naïve
unfeeling	pessimistic	adolescent	pedantic	cynical	epicurean
hot-headed	unpunctual	long-winded	short-sighted	critical	insecure
selfish	undisciplined	unfaithful	boastful	moralizing	gullible
ruthless	dissatisfied	untruthful	mistrustful	stubborn	defenceless
tactless	irresponsible	untrustworthy	extravagant	defensive	non-competitive
impatient					earthy
rebellious					
Buzz Aldrin	Mick Jagger	Yul Brynner	Katharine Hepburn	Winston Churchill	Al Capone
Neil Armstrong	Joni Mitchell	many comedians	many military officers	Elvis Presley	Lucille Ball
Paul Simon				Sophia Loren	Elton John
Paul McCartney				Brigitte Bardot	Humphrey Bogart
Jimi Hendrix					Alfred Hitchcock

EXAMPLE 53d[13]

This game can be played either in class or in a group. The idea is to make a set of words beginning with the same given group of letters.

  The teacher, or someone in the group, reads out from the dictionary five definitions of words which all begin, for example, with the letters COM:

(i)	Official group of people who decide/organise	COMMITTEE
(ii)	Ordinary/happening very frequently	COMMON
(iii)	Person who travels/lives with someone	COMPANION
(iv)	business firm	COMPANY
(v)	Whole/with all parts	COMPLETE

4.1.5 Semantics: Denotation and connotation

Three ways of teaching word meanings (denotation) are synonymy, antonymy and definition (see sections 1.2 and 2.2). Here are some exercises with avoid these in isolation, providing some limiting context at least (Examples 54a−d).

EXAMPLE 54a[15]

1a There's a lot of *sense* in what children say about their parents.

    A feeling **B** wisdom **C** meaning **D** normal state of mind

b Officers should have a *sense* of responsibility when taking serious military decisions.

    A feeling **B** wisdom **C** meaning **D** power of judgement

2a He fell asleep *while* reading a boring book.

    A whereas **B** although **C** during the time of **D** as long as

2b *While* he isn't very bright, he nevertheless works well.

    A whereas **B** although **C** during the time of **D** as long as

3a The speaker *gathered* a crowd round him.

    A obtained **B** brought together **C** understood **D** hoarded

3b From what the minister said, we *gathered* that there were going to be cuts in the budget.

    A obtained **B** brought together **C** understood **D** hoard

3c Before you are accepted for this job you must *gather* a bit more experience.

    A obtain   **B** bring together   **C** understand   **D** hoard

4a Many people emigrate to *seek* their fortune elsewhere.

    A look for   **B** ask   **C** try   **D** follow

4b The kidnappers *sought* to blackmail the rich businessman.

    A looked for   **B** asked   **C** tried   **D** followed

5a The scholar *framed* his theory on the basis of experimental data.

    A built   **B** put a frame round   **C** developed   **D** invented

5b The parents *framed* the photograph of their child.

    A built   **B** put a frame round   **C** developed   **D** invented

6a He couldn't bear the *prospect* of his sister's marriage.

    A expectation   **B** vision   **C** chance   **D** outlook

6b The doctors couldn't see much *prospect* of the patient's recovery.

    A expectation   **B** vision   **C** chance   **D** outlook

7a Our argument had no *effect* on their firm decision.

    A outcome   **B** influence   **C** impression   **D** event

EXAMPLE 54b[15]

Opposites

Write down the word which means the opposite in these sentences.

1 Ted isn't *good-looking*. He's _____.
2 First, *open* the door. Then _____ it.
3 That is the *wrong* road. Do you know the _____ one?
4 One man can *push* and the other can _____.
5 This place isn't *safe*. It's _____.
6 The boat isn't *empty*. It's _____.
7 The work isn't *easy*. It's _____.
8 The boat *arrives* at the Falls in the morning and it _____ in the evening.
9 The music is *soft*. It isn't _____.

EXAMPLE 54c[15]

Break

'Break' forms several two/three-word verbs. Here is an extract from the *Oxford Dictionary of Current Idiomatic English*: Volume I: This extract looks at uses of 'break' with 'in' and 'into'. Only 'break in²ˑ (B) is separable.

A   **break in**[1] [A1] interrupt. **S:** speaker, critic. **A:** sharply, abruptly, excitedly □ *'But what's going to happen to us?'* *one of the miners* **broke in**. □ *normally precedes or follows direct speech.*

B   **break in**[2] [B1 i pass] accustom to new discipline, make docile; make soft and pliable. **S:** trainer, drill sergeant. **O:** horse, mount; recruit, novice; pair of boots □ *Petruccchio* **broke in** *a shrewish wife.* □ *New recruits are often* **broken in** *by repeated drilling on the barrack square.*

C   **break in/into** [A1 nom A2 pass adj] force an entry (into), force one's way in(to). **S:** burglar, intruder. **o:** shop, private house, warehouse □ *Tell them that those inside need protection against desperate characters who are trying to* **break in** *from outside.* TBC □ *There was a* **break-in** *at Smith's warehouse.* □ *Stores were* **broken into** *and looted during the riots.*

D   **break in on/upon** [A3 pass emph rel] interrupt, disturb. **S:** noise, voice, **O:** thinking, meditation, conversation □ *A sudden noise from outside* **broke in upon** *his day-dream.* □ *Their meeting was* **broken in upon** *by the arrival of a group of petitioners.*

E   **break into**[1] [A2] suddenly change from a slower to a faster pace. **S:** horse, elephant, herd. **o:** ▽ a run, trot,

canter, gallop □ *As soon as they scented water, the whole herd* **broke into** *a gallop.* □ *'I shall be late'* − *she was on the point of* **breaking into** *a run.* PW

F   **break into**[2] [A2] suddenly begin to laugh etc. **S:** audience, crowd. **o:** (loud) laughter, song, cheers □ *As the President's car appeared, the waiting crowds* **broke into** *loud cheers.*

G   **break into**[3] [A2 pass] take time from, encroach on/upon (q v). **S:** overtime, extra duties, nightwork. **o:** evenings, leisure time □ *'I can't take on any extra overtime: my weekends have been* **broken into** *far too much as it is.'*

H   **break into**[4] [A2 pass] use a high-value note or coin to buy an article costing less. **S:** customer, purchaser, **o:** pound note, ten-dollar bill □ *'I can't give you the forty pence I owe you without* **breaking into** *a five-pound note, so do you mind if I pay you back tomorrow?'*

I   **break into**[5] [A2 pass] open and consume (sth held in reserve for emergency use). **S:** garrison, beleaguered population, expedition. **o:** (reserve stocks of) water, food, ammunition; iron-rations □ *The stranded party* **broke into** *their emergency supplies of food and water.*

J   **break into**[6] [A2 pass adj] force an entry into ⇒ break in/into.

Exercise 2

Read these sentences, and note which meaning (A–J) you think is being used.

1 New shoes are often uncomfortable until you've broken them in. ☐

2 'Hold on, I'll just find some change. I don't want to break into a ten pound note.' ☐

3 'Come back tomorrow and . . .' 'I can't wait that long,' broke in Mark, 'I've got to see him today.' ☐

4 I was trying to keep a straight face, but when he fell over the wastepaper bin I just broke into roars of laughter. ☐

5 I was trying to work, when the noise of a cassette-player blasting out music broke in on me. ☐

6 When they saw the bus coming, they broke into a run. ☐

7 Look I know you're busy. Do you mind if I just break in on you for a moment. ☐

8 They broke in through an upstairs window which the owners had forgotten to close. ☐

9 'We've run out of milk. We'll have to break into the reserve supply again.' 'But we keep that for an emergency!' ☐

10 That's the trouble with the night-shift. It breaks into your private life too much. ☐

E Reading

The Home Tool Box

Read the article and then match the tools in the picture with the descriptions.

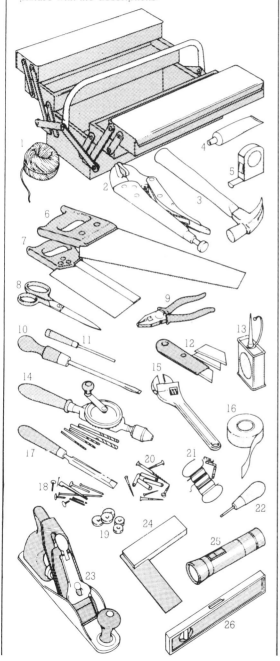

D.I.Y. SPECIAL

EVERY HOME'S TOOL KIT

There are some tools that no home should be without. Even the simplest repair job is difficult if you have not got the right tools. You can store them in a plastic or metal tool box so that they are always at hand. The most important tools are as follows:

- [ ] A metric steel *tape measure* for measuring things accurately.
- [ ] A *tenon saw* which has small teeth and is very easy to use when you want to saw small pieces of wood.
- [ ] A *panel saw* for larger pieces of wood.
- [ ] A heavy *claw hammer*. The claw is useful for pulling nails out.
- [ ] *Pliers* for bending, twisting, stripping and cutting wire as well as for holding small objects.
- [ ] An *electric screwdriver* for changing plugs and replacing fuses. The handle is insulated to protect you against electric shocks.
- [ ] A *large screwdriver* for putting screws into wood and for lifting paint lids off.
- [ ] A *Stanley knife* with different blades for cutting linoleum and carpet.
- [ ] A *hand drill* with different bits to match your wall plugs, for drilling holes in the walls and in wood.
- [ ] *Insulating tape* for covering bare electric wire and repairing pipes.
- [ ] *Fuse wire* (5 amp, 15 amp, 30 amp) and *fuses* (3 amp, 13 amp) for repairing fuse boxes and plugs.
- [ ] A set of different sized *screws* and *rawlplugs*.
- [ ] Assorted *nails* and *tacks*.
- [ ] A *bradawl* for making holes in things, especially for screws.
- [ ] A *smoothing plane* for making wood smooth. Alternatively have some different grades of glasspaper in the tool box for the same purpose.
- [ ] *Tap washers*, big for the bath taps and small for the other taps.
- [ ] A can of penetrating *oil* for clearing rust from metal, for oiling doors, etc.
- [ ] A *torch* for working in the dark.
- [ ] An *adjustable spanner* for undoing all sizes of nuts.
- [ ] A *spirit level* for making shelves exactly horizontal.
- [ ] A *set square* for making a perfect right angle.

- [ ] You can also have *glue* for sticking things, a
- [ ] *wrench* for holding objects very tightly and a
- [ ] *chisel* for cutting away small pieces of wood.
- [ ][ ] *String* and a pair of *scissors* are also useful.

Examples 54e and 54f show how the denotation of abstract words can be taught imaginatively:

EXAMPLE 54e

Coins Speak

Assemble a collection of identical small objects, e.g. counters, coins, buttons: you will need around 10 per student.

Make sure you have plenty of plain white paper, A4 size or larger.

Prepare a list or lists of words you would like the students to work on: these should be words of a strong emotional content, or with a marked conceptual or controversial flavour, e.g.

GUILT   INDEPENDENCE   INNOCENCE   REVENGE

Ask the students to form groups of 2–3.

Ask one student in each group to select a word from the list and then, without saying which word s/he has chosen, to represent the word by means of an arrangement of counters or coins on the paper.

When the first student has done this, the others in the group should try to guess which word was selected.

Examples:

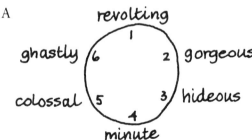

MISERY: one is excluded   SADNESS: tears falling
       from the group   from eye

EXAMPLE 54f[15]

Suggested procedure: On the blackboard draw two circles and add the vocabulary thus:

A

revolting
1

ghastly 6   2 *gorgeous*

colossal 5   3 *hideous*

4
minute

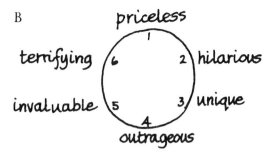

B

priceless

terrifying 6

2 hilarious

invaluable 5

3 unique

4

outrageous

Divide the students into small groups and give each group a dice. All groups do the following activity at the same time.

One student in each group throws the dice twice; the first throw corresponds to dial A and the second to dial B. If, for example, he throws 5 the first time and 6 the second, his two words are 'colossal' and 'terrifying'. The group then has to make a note of the two words and think of something or someone which includes these two words in their meaning (e.g. King Kong). The next student in the group takes his turn to throw the dice and the groups thus build up a set of about five to six two-word combinations and an example for each.

Now bring the whole class together, and ask the first group to tell their example (i.e. King Kong). The rest of the class then have to decide which two adjectives from the circles were the ones they had thrown.

Connotation is the teaching point of the exercises in Examples 55a−e:

EXAMPLE 55a[16]

Write down the word in each of the following sentences which shows that the writer is being derogatory.
(i)   He has an antiquated car.
(ii) His wife is a calculating woman.
(iii) He is a callow youth.
(iv) I wish you'd stop dithering.
(v)   I had forgotten that she was so dumpy.

EXAMPLE 55b[16]

Reading

The Advertising Standards Authority controls advertising in Britain. Read some of these extracts from their *Code of Practice*.

Appendix M
Advertising of cigarettes and hand-rolling tobacco

RULES

2.1 Advertisements should not exaggerate the attractions of smoking or otherwise seek to persuade people to start smoking.

2.2 Advertisements should not seek to encourage smokers to smoke more or to smoke to excess or show a cigarette left in the mouth.

2.3 Advertisements should not exploit those who are especially vulnerable, whether on account of their youth or immaturity or as a result of any physical, mental or social handicap.

2.4 Advertisements should not claim directly or indirectly that it is natural to smoke, or that it is abnormal not to smoke.

2.5 Advertisements should not claim directly or indirectly any health advantage of one brand over other brands except on evidence which has been accepted by the health authorities.

2.6 Advertisements should not claim directly or indirectly that smoking is a necessity for relaxation or for concentration.

2.7 Advertisements should not claim directly or indirectly that to smoke, or to smoke a particular brand, is a sign or proof of manliness, courage or daring.

2.8 Advertisements should not include or imply any personal testimonial for, or recommendation of the product by any well-known person of distinction in any walk of life, nor should they claim directly or indirectly the recommendation of a particular brand by any group or class of people engaged in an activity or calling which particularly attracts public admiration or emulation.

2.9 Advertisements should not include copy or illustrations which are sexually titilating or which imply a link between smoking and sexual success, nor should any advertisement contain any demonstration of affection in such a way as to suggest romantic or sexual involvement between those portrayed.

2.10 Advertisements should not claim directly or indirectly that it contributes singificantly to the attainment of social or business success to smoke, or to smoke a particular brand.

2.11 No advertisement for cigarettes should appear in any publication directed wholly or mainly to young people.

2.12 Advertisements should not feature heroes of the young.

Exercise

The ASA is also concerned with the use of language in advertising. The use of the words 'free' and 'guaranteed', for example, are strictly controlled. The authority however admits that words like 'best' and 'finest' have become so devalued that they can be used in advertising. Imagine you are creating an advertisement. Which words would you choose for these sentences?

1 The lipstick is
   a cherry red
   b crimson
   c blood red.

2 The eye-shadow is
   a black diamond
   b coal black
   c sooty.

3 The cigar has a strong
   a aroma
   b smell
   c odour
   d stink.

4 This jacket is especially suitable for men who are
   a fat
   b stout
   c well-built

5 The new alcoholic drink is
   a sharp-tasting
   b acid
   c dry.

EXAMPLE 55c¹⁶

5 ♦♦♦♦

> What sort of person is he?

Make three lists from the words on the left: one with good characteristics, one with bad characteristics and one with characteristics which are not good or bad. *Compare your lists with another group.*

6

Which of the words in exercise 5 can you use to describe:
your mother or father?
your brother or sister or friend?
yourself?

EXAMPLE 55d¹⁶

Look at the following list of adjectives and underline the 8 which describe the negative aspects of housework:

uncongenial/challenging/fascinating/damaging/rewarding/non-specialised/
dead-end/isolating/status-degrading/absorbing/stimulating/fulfilling/menial/
unpaid.

EXAMPLE 55e¹⁶

Good Words   Bad Words

Tell the students that when you learn a foreign language you meet words you like and words you don't, words you remember straight off and words you don't. Give some examples from your own foreign language learning. (Allow 2–3 minutes only for this introduction.)

Give the students the words to be reviewed and ask them each to pick three they like and three they don't. Give them time to think.

Put up two headings on the board:

nice words   nasty words

Ask each student to write up *one* of his/her nice words and *one* nasty word.

When everybody has two words on the board incite people to explain why they like/don't like their particular word. Do not gloss and comment yourself: don't give or withhold approval. By keeping quiet you will help the students to talk.

Examples

In one group of students the review words were:

> viaduct/ambulance/to lower/motorway/plunge/jack-knife/to volunteer/
> hair-raising/jelly/windscreen/intensive.

Here are some of the things different students said about some of the words:

ambulance: 'I used to be a nurse and an ambulance coming mean more work. I don't like the word.'

intensive: 'I don't like it because *nt* is too hard for to say correctly.'

jelly: 'I like it. The sound is right.'

windscreen: 'I don't like it because I learnt it last term and I can't remember it.'

4.1.6 Polysemy and the relationship of sound to spelling

Polysemy (cf. section 1.2) is the subject of these two exercises from *Learning with LDOCE* (Examples 56a and b):

EXAMPLE 56a[17]

Look up each pair of words in the dictionary, and then arrange them in three columns, like this:

same pronunciation	different pronunciation and stress	different pronunciation
earnest	conduct	

You will notice that an unstressed syllable often contains the sound ɪ or ə. Read *Pronunciation* paragraph 6.3.1.p. xviii.

1. There were TEARS in her eyes.
   There were TEARS in his trousers.
2. Have you signed the CONTRACT?
   Metal will CONTRACT as its temperature falls.
3. I want a LEAD pencil.
   He is to LEAD the orchestra.
4. She is lovely beyond COMPARE.
   Please COMPARE these two photographs.
5. This machine RECORDS the force of the wind.
   Come and hear my new RECORDS.

6. This is the woman THAT shot him.
    THAT's the man she shot.
7. I could ADVANCE you £10.
    Would you like an ADVANCE of £10?
8. There's not much PROSPECT of winning.
    He went to Australia to PROSPECT for gold.
9. You need a PERMIT to enter.
    This card will PERMIT you to enter.
10. Just wait a MINUTE.
    He described the event in MINUTE detail.
11. I can't hear with the ROW going on.
    They're all sitting in a ROW.
12. Do you SEPARATE the boys from the girls?
    Do the boys and the girls work in SEPARATE rooms?

EXAMPLE 56b[17]

Things and ideas

Words with several meanings

Find out from the dictionary which of the words in CAPITALS will fit into the first set of sentences, then which word will fit into the second set, and so on:

CROSS   KEY   POST   SKIM   EYE

1. Here's the ... for winding up the clock. Look up the answers in the ... at the back. One of the ...s of the typewriter is stuck.
2. I've got a fly in my .... Push the thread through the ... of the needle. You certainly have a good ... for a bargain!
3. Always ... the cream off the milk. I watched the ball ... past my head. He only had time to ... through the chapter.
4. Just ... the street and turn right. You should ... the cheque when you've signed it. We're hoping to ... these two breeds of cattle.
5. I'll send your shoes by .... The sentry fell asleep at his .... He tied his horse to a convenient ....

We are familiar with crosswords used as spelling practice. The following spelling exercises are on the theme of anagrams, but they all provide a limiting context for the learner (Examples 57a−c). In 57a the anagrams are paired with pictures; in 57b they are all places; and in 57c when one anagram is guessed, it is relatively easy to find the others:

EXAMPLE 57a[18]

Can you spell these?

1 SOTPEOAT

2 RYRLO

3 NIOOSN

4 HOMOMUSSR

5 SPOSAPTR

6 HRCTO

EXAMPLE 57b[18]

1   Places

Spell names of places with these letters.

Example: NATOTIS = station

1   KANB   . . . .

2   STOPFFIEOC   . . . .

3   TESTAURAANR   . . . .

4   NATOTISSUB   . . . .

5   CAIEMN   . . . .

6   ATIRORP   . . . .

EXAMPLE 57c[18]

Rearrange the letters of the word in the middle and find the name of a very popular invention. All the other words are connected with it.

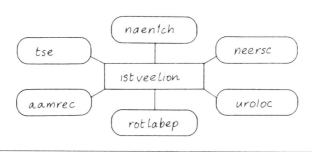

The three spelling puzzles below (Examples 58a−c) encourage figure/ground discrimination, since there is no white space to indicate where word beginnings and endings lie:

EXAMPLE 58a[19]

C3 Find the other months of the year!

```
F U D C M H N A T X U O V D C S
A F X O P Q A S M V Z C E F H A
O M I J X P J E U F L T Q T D L
F I M U P L U R T X A O B O E L
D Z O N P I L M A Y C B F G C Y
U B T E S Z Y P U M J E H T E Q
O L Q X A D Z Y G S U R N T M S
R M S T N E N V U Q M B J X B A
D S E B G S O S S T A O A B E I
U A P R I L V S T B G E N C R R
S M T Y P Z E V A L G T U O N A
D P E V T X M W D W I M A R C H
A S M O Z S B T P S E G R A B P
V I B N A F E B R U A R Y L W U
E D E N P Q R U S E W O T I G T
T R R E S R G T X I Y M O E S R
```

EXAMPLE 58b[19]

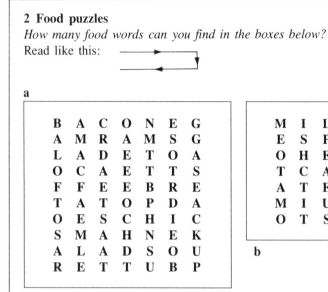

2 Food puzzles
How many food words can you find in the boxes below?
Read like this:

a

```
B  A  C  O  N  E  G          M  I  L  K  S  U  G
A  M  R  A  M  S  G          E  S  P  A  N  C  A
L  A  D  E  T  O  A          O  H  E  E  S  A  R
O  C  A  E  T  T  S          T  C  A  D  E  K  B
F  F  E  E  B  R  E          A  T  E  R  B  E  I
T  A  T  O  P  D  A          M  I  U  R  F  S  S
O  E  S  C  H  I  C          O  T  S  T  I  U  C
S  M  A  H  N  E  K
A  L  A  D  S  O  U          b
R  E  T  T  U  B  P
```

EXAMPLE 58c[19]

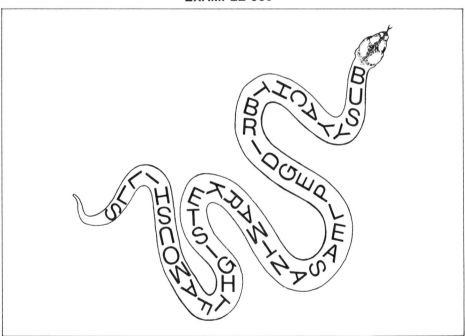

Spelling can be improved by playing games such as Scrabble,[20] Boggle or Lexicon, whilst at elementary level the Debden Suffix Changing Cards by K. Hadley or the Cromwell Word Meaning Activities by John Baguley may be useful (both available from Philip and Tacey). The former has four sets of eight suffix cards such as `-ning` `-ting` and `-ping` , which must be placed alongside corresponding word beginnings, such as `can-` `fit-` and `dip-` . The latter is another matching activity, this time using initial blends, printed on orange cards, to which other cards are added to complete the words, for example `sw` `ing` , `wh` `en` , `str` `ong` .

One aspect of the relationship between sound and spelling is the occurrence of weak forms due to shifting stress patterns in connected speech. New lexical items can be marked for stress by underlining, by having the prominent syllable in bold type, or by using upper case characters. Tricia Hedge[21] gives advice to students making their own vocabulary books, suggesting that alongside the L1 equivalent, an example, a synonym and some indication of its morphology, they should mark each new item for stress in one of three ways:

Method 1	**Method 2**	**Method 3**
import	ímport	import
imagination	imaginátion	imagination
cigarette	cigarétte	cigarette
depart	depárt	depart

The following exercise (Example 59a) makes learners aware of the shift in stress which happens when words of identical spelling have different grammatical functions:

EXAMPLE 59a[22]

Stress shift

*** Words or phrases marked /*/ are pronounced with a different stress pattern when they come before
    a noun. Read the following sentences or expressions aloud, and then copy out each word in CAPITALS
    twice, marking the correct main stress as it would be said in each of the two expressions.

    Example: He went UPSTAIRS.
                    an UPSTAIRS room
    Answer: **up´stairs, ´upstairs**

    1.   She went to UNIVERSITY.
          the UNIVERSITY library
    2.   UP TO DATE information
          Bring me UP TO DATE.
    3.   an Italian PRINCESS
          PRINCESS Mary
    4.   She's very INDEPENDENT.
          an INDEPENDENT decision
    5.   Are you LEFT-HANDED?
          LEFT-HANDED scissors

4.1.7 Mother tongue transfer

It is now generally accepted that language learners will make comparisons between their own language and the target language, whether their teacher encourages this or not. There will always be items in the target language which have similar sound to those in the L1, sometimes humorously so, and such similarities can be exploited as *aides-mémoire*.[23] The key word method of vocabulary teaching, which makes systematic use of the L1, may be of use at elementary level. For example, the word *ei* in German means *egg* in English, and the two words can be visually represented thus:

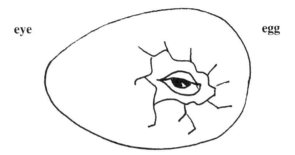

The Translation Game from Morgan and Rinvolucri, *Learning English Words*, makes use of the mother tongue as in Example 59b:

EXAMPLE 59b[24]

Ensure that each member of the group has access to a bilingual dictionary. Write up an English word on the blackboard (one which will produce a rich set of translations).

  Ask the students to work individually to look up in the dictionary the word you have put up. They choose one of the dictionary translations and look that up in the other section of the dictionary. They then look one of these translations up...and so on.

  Working with a German—English dictionary one student produced this list:

  Bag Sack Laufpass Dismissal Entlassung Release Befriegung
  Deliverance Rettung Salvage Bergung Sheltering Zufhict
  Refuge

Some teachers may be taken aback by the kind of blatant use of bilingual dictionaries advocated in the above exercise. Many frown on the use of any dictionary in class, believing that learners should try to deduce meaning from context. Della Summers[25] holds the view that looking up a word in a dictionary demands its own skill: tracing an inflected verb form back to its base form, for example. She also makes the point that there are occasions when meaning is simply *not* deducible from context, as in her own example of 'dratted' in this sentence:

She had always made Pippin laugh: she would miss her and her *dratted* every-lasting reminiscing.

Bilingual dictionaries are used in the initial stages of learning a language, but we need to help our learners make the shift to monolingual dictionaries as their proficiency increases.[26] We can set simple questions to make learners comfortable with handling these, and with finding words they have never encountered before. There are examples from dictionary workbooks given in this volume, and here are a few more ideas which can help integrate dictionary work into general English lessons:

1. Use the dictionary for simple work on alphabetical order, e.g. 'What's the next word in your dictionary after "fish"?'
2. Use the dictionary for finding out meanings quickly, with multiple choice questions, e.g. 'What's an "aardvark"? An insect, a bird or an animal?'
3. Use the dictionary for work on grammar by introducing some of its grammatical symbols and making them the basis of exercises, e.g. for the symbols (v) and (n), 'Are these words verbs or nouns' irritant/irritate/barter/garter?'
4. Use the dictionary for work on pronunciation of a difficult sound, e.g. for /ʃ/ ask learners to look up 'reassure', 'pressure', 'artificial', 'station', as well as the more usual words which begin with the sound, such as 'sugar' and 'shoulder'. This should help towards an understanding of the fact that a one-to-one relationship between sound and spelling does not always exist in English.
5. Use the dictionary for fun in word games, e.g. finding adjectives for each letter of the alphabet to complete the sentence:

'I love my love with an "a" (and so on) because she's . . .'

One of my students' first three responses were:

'I love my love with an"a" because she's agreeable;
I love my love with a "b" because she's buxom;
I love my love with a "c" because she's crazy.'.

Learners have a tendency to look for direct translations of unknown words, and where these do not exist an EFL dictionary can help. This is a dictionary specifically designed for foreign learners of English in which definitions are expressed in simple controlled vocabulary, examples in context are given, and there are explanations of grammar. Many[27] give information too on cultural factors which may affect a speaker's choice of vocabulary, such as whether he feels himself superior, inferior or equal to his hearer.[28]

Research by Longman[29] has shown that whilst native English speakers use dictionaries to look up uncommon words or those which are often confused, learners look up more frequent words, especially abstract ones. We owe it to our learners to train them in dictionary use, so that they can move away from dependence on us towards autonomy and self-instruction. However, we also owe it to our learners to help them choose their dictionaries wisely: the point was made earlier (section 4.1.2) that words capable of both a general and a specific meaning cause the most problems for learners of ESP. A glance at the entries for 'issue' below shows the danger of recommending specialist dictionaries which may not concern themselves with the more general meaning. The converse is also true, i.e. that learners may use a general EFL dictionary when searching for a word capable of a very specific sense, such as 'resistance' in the context of electricity. Try looking up 'resistance' in a few dictionaries to which you have access and see whether both general and specific meanings are given! The new emphasis on vocabulary teaching may bring with it a greater use of dictionaries in the classroom and more instruction in how to exploit the information they contain.

EXAMPLE 59c

Issue

Harrap's 2000 Word: no entry

Chambers First Learner's:

['iʃuː]
issue   a result; a problem. The same word also
        means to send or give something out.

Chambers Dictionary of Science and Technology: no entry

Oxford Elementary Learner's:

issue /'ɪʃuː/ *v.* **1** come or go out of somewhere: *Smoke was issuing from the chimney.* **2** give something out to someone: *Please issue everyone with a pencil.*

Longman Dictionary of Scientific Usage:

AF098 issue (*v.i.*) To come out or to flow out from a place; the term usually implies coming out of an opening, *e.g.* wait until steam issues freely before connecting the apparatus □ *water issues from a tap*—***issue*** (*n.*) ↓ EMANATE (Sn) · EMERGE (Sn) · OOZE · EXUDE ↑ ORIGINATE

Evans Learner's Dictionary of Science and Technology:

issue
/'ɪsjuː/   *vi* To come out: *Water issued from the pipe.*

Jones/Gimson Pronouncing Dictionary:

iss|ue (*s. v.*), **-ues, -uing, -ued, -uer/s;**
-uable, -uance 'ıʃ|uː ['ısj|uː, 'ıʃj|uː],
-uːz, -uːɪŋ [-ʊɪŋ], -uːd, -uːə* [-ʊə*]/z;
-uːəbl [-ʊəbl], -uːəns [-ʊəns]

Oxford English Picture Dictionary: no entry

Collins Cobuild English Language Dictionary:

issue /ɪʃuː/, **issues, issuing, issued.** 1 An **issue** N COUNT : USU + is an important subject that people are discussing or SUPP arguing about. EG *People should let their MPs know* = matter *where they stand on this issue... This has not been raised as an issue by the West... ...the issues at stake... ...an important and serious issue... ...social issues.*
2 When you talk about **the issue**, you are referring to N SING : the + N the really important part of the thing that you are = the point considering or discussing. EG *That's just not the issue... What I think of you simply isn't the issue.*
3 The point **at issue**, question **at issue**, etc is the PHR : USED AS AN most important part of something that you are A, OR NG + PHR considering or discussing. EG *The point at issue is* = in question *this... It was the content of literacy studies that was at issue... What is at issue is the extent to which inflation causes unemployment.*
4 If you **evade the issue**, **duck the issue**, etc, you PHR : VB refuse to accept or deal with an important problem INFLECTS or a difficult subject; used showing disapproval. EG = prevaricate *You can no longer go on evading the issue... Congress ducked the issue... He was skirting the issue.*
5 If you **cloud the issue**, **confuse the issue**, etc, you PHR : VB introduce unimportant matters into a discussion or INFLECTS conversation, preventing people from paying attention to the main subject; used showing disapproval. EG *Her explanations usually just clouded the issue... Let's not confuse the issue.*
6 An **issue** is also a reason for quarrelling or N COUNT : USU disagreement. EG *If you'd stayed at home, we* SING *wouldn't have had an issue... He stood up, deter-* ⇑ difference *mined to settle the issue between them finally and at* = argument *once.*
7 If you **make an issue of something**, you make an PHR : VB unnecessary fuss about it; used showing disapproval. INFLECTS EG *She didn't want to make an issue of it... Some parents make such an issue of adoption.*

8 If you **take issue with** someone or **take issue with** PHR : VB something that they have said, you disagree with INFLECTS what they have said, and start arguing about it. EG *I* ⇑ contradict *was bold enough to take issue with the director... I want to take issue with John Taylor about his ideas on illegitimacy... I would take issue with that.*
9 An **issue** is also 9.1 a particular edition of a N COUNT magazine, newspaper, etc. EG *We sell 2,000 copies per issue... The article had appeared in the previous day's issue.* 9.2 the result or outcome of something; a N SING : a + ADJ + formal or literary use. EG *He wants his prayers to* N *have a prosperous issue... He was on the way to insure a happy issue for their love.*
10 Your child or children can be referred to as your N UNCOUNT **issue**; a legal or old-fashioned use. EG *He died without* = progeny *issue.*
11 If you **issue** a statement, warning, etc, you make V + O it formally or publicly. EG *We considered issuing* = send out *some sort of statement or press release... They issued a serious warning... We issued a formal invitation from this department.*
12 If you **issue** something or if you issue someone V + O : IF + PREP with it, you officially provide or equip them with it. THEN *with* EG *We were issued with a set of instructions?... Who* ⇑ supply *issued the travel documents?... I was issued with a new rifle.* ▸ used as a noun. EG *The issue of firearms...* ▸ N UNCOUNT *It is illegal for a soldier to retain any piece of war* ⇑ provision *issue.*
13 If you **issue** a document, you officially produce it V + O : IF + PREP and make it available. EG *The Ministry had to cancel* THEN *to* *plans to issue government bonds.* ▸ used as a noun. ▸ N UNCOUNT/ EG *...the issue of commemorative stamps.* COUNT
14 When a liquid, sound, smell, etc **issues** from V + A (from) something, it comes out of it. EG *There were caves,* = emerge *with streams issuing from them... ...the smells issuing from the back kitchen... Mr Hughes's voice, issuing from the darkness, sounded loud and frightening.*

Longman Dictionary of Contemporary English:

is·sue[1] /'ıʃuː, 'ısjuː‖'ıʃuː/ *n* 1 [C] a subject to be talked about, argued about, or decided: *Parliament will debate the nationalization issue next week.* | *one of the key issues in the election campaign* | *I don't want to* **make an issue of it.** (=quarrel about it) 2 [C] something which is produced so as to be publicly sold or given out: *The Christmas issue of the magazine had a picture of carol singers on its cover.* | *There's a new issue of stamps to commemorate the Royal Wedding.* 3 [U] the act of coming out or being produced: *I bought the new stamp the day of its issue.* | (*fml*) the issue of blood from a wound 4 [U + *sing./pl. v*] old use and law children (esp. in the phrase **die without issue**) 5 [C] *fml* what happens in the end; the result: *to await the issue* 6 **at issue** under consideration, esp. because of some doubt: *Her ability is*

not at issue; it's her character I'm worried about. 7 **take issue with** *fml* to disagree with (a person) —see also RIGHT ISSUE, SIDE ISSUE
issue[2] *v* [T] 1 to produce (esp. something printed and/ or official): *Banknotes of this design were first issued 20 years ago.* | *The government is expected to issue a statement about the crisis.* 2 to give out or provide officially: *Our new uniforms haven't been issued yet.* [+ *obj* + **with**] *They issued the firemen with breathing equipment.* [+ *obj* + *to*] *They issued breathing equipment to the firemen.*
issue forth *phr v* [I] *lit* to go or come out
issue from sthg. *phr v* [T *no pass.*] *fml* to come or result from: *smoke issuing from the chimneys* | *Our economic problems issue from a lack of investment.*

4.2 Tasks

Group tasks

1. Look at the following headlines, which appeared on the same day in four different British newspapers, reporting the same story.[30] Arrange them in order from most formal to least formal, and then discuss why you have arranged them in that way. (Possible questions to ask yourselves are: How is the vocabulary simplified? Do the words become shorter? Does the language become more personal?):

    (a) **WIDOW OF TUBE FIRE HERO GETS £250,000**

    (b) **£250,000 FOR A HERO'S LIFE**

    (c) **£250,000 FOR WIDOW OF KING'S CROSS HERO**

    (d) **DAMAGES FOR TUBE FIREMAN'S WIDOW**

2. Take a large sheet of paper and coloured pens for each group and 'brainstorm' your group's connections for the following words (look again at the example for 'friend' in this chapter):

    FEAR   PRODUCE

3. Think of a few idioms/proverbs/fixed expressions from your own language. Translate them word for word into English, and discuss the meaning they now convey (if any!). Are there any idioms in English which are equivalent in meaning? Use the list you have made with your classes as a way of raising their awareness of cultural differences.

4. Form small groups to devise a crossword puzzle, word search or game to practise a spelling difficulty or difficulties which your learners might experience when writing in English. Then exchange puzzles with the other groups and try them out.

Self-assessed tasks

1. The following sentences are from three separate articles written on the same subject.[30] Your task is to reconstitute the original three articles by choosing the most appropriate sentence from each numbered group, in the order given. For example, if you think that the best sentence to follow (a)(i) is (b)(ii) then write them in that sequence, and so on.

    (a) (i)   The widow of King's Cross hero fireman Colin Townsley finally received £250,000 damages from London Underground yesterday.

        (ii) The widow of Mr Colin Townsley, the fireman who died in the King's Cross fire, was awarded damages of £250,000 in the High Court yesterday.

        (iii) The widow of King's Cross fireman Colin Townsley was awared £250,000 damages yesterday.

(b) (i) Mrs Linda Townsley looked strained and repeatedly turned her wedding ring as the High Court heard how her husband 'died a hero's death' in the 1987 Tube inferno.

(ii) The award to Mrs Linda Townsley, which was approved by Mr Justice Michael Davies, is a record for a fireman killed on duty.

(iii) Mrs Linda Townsley took her case to the High Court to force a settlement for the November 1987 tragedy in which 31 died.

(c) (i) As toxic smoke filled the Underground Station he turned back from a chance to escape to help a badly burned woman.

(ii) After the hearing in London her Solicitor, Mr Andrew Dismore, strongly criticised the Underground for 'intransigence' which he said had caused Mrs Townsley many months of worry and uncertainty.

(iii) Part of the award was made in respect of the 'minutes of terror' the senior fireman suffered when he collapsed from the fumes and was waiting to be enveloped by the fireball that killed a total of 31 people.

(d) (i) Station Officer Townsley 'suffered some minutes of terror of impending death' as he suffocated in a tunnel, said Benet Hytner QC.

(ii) Mr Benet Hytner QC, for Mrs Townsley, paid tribute to the man who had 'died a hero's death'.

(iii) 'London Underground held out to the last minute — the negotiations were concluded only 3 weeks ago' he said.

2. You are preparing to read a text of about 200 words on the subject of a girl's first few weeks at secondary school, called 'The First Year'. Try to predict up to twenty vocabulary items which will occur in the text. Make a list of them, and check with the key whether you were successful in your predictions.

3. Match the prefixes and suffixes from column A with their corresponding meaning from column B:[31]

A   B

(a) able (i) Added to some verbs that describe processes in order to form verbs describing the opposite processes.

(b) ish (ii) Added to uncount nouns to form adjectives describing something as being in a particular state.

(c) un (iii) Added to adjectives to form other adjectives describing something as having a particular property, quality or colour, but only to a certain extent.

(d) ify (iv) Added to adjectives, adverbs and nouns in order to form words that have the opposite meaning.

(e) dis (v) In verbs that refer to the putting of something or someone into a particular state or condition.

(f) or (vi) Added to adjectives and nouns to form other adjectives and nouns which refer to something existing or happening between similar things or groups of people.

(g) inter(vii)In nouns that refer to people who do a particular type of work, or a
          particular type of action.
4.   Each of the pictures which follow should give you a clue to the anagram contained
     within it. Can you solve them?

Notes and references

1   Such lists include M. West, *General Service List*, Thorndike-Lorge, 1953; *A Teachers' Handbook
    of 30,000 words*, 1944; and R. Hindmarsh, *The Cambridge English Lexicon*, Cambridge
    University Press, 1980.
2. P. Moore and M. Skinner, in their article 'The effects of illustrations on children's comprehension
    of abstract and concrete passages', *Journal of Research in Reading* 1985, **8(1)**: 45–56, describe
    improved reading comprehension in every one of the children studied. The interesting finding
    here was that *abstract* passages were made easier to understand by the use of pictures.
3. Example 45a is from T. Hedge, *Using Readers in Language Teaching*, Macmillan, 1985.
4. Example 45b is from R. Gairns and S. Redman, *Working with Words*, Cambridge University
    Press, 1986.
5. Example 46 is from J. McGrath, unpublished project presented in part fulfilment of the MA
    in Applied Linguistics, University of Birmingham, 1986.
6. Example 47 is from E. Kirkpatrick, *Chambers Universal Learners' Dictionary Workbook*,
    Chambers, 1981.
7. C. Kennedy and R. Bolitho, *English for Specific Purposes*, Macmillan, 1984.
8. Example 48a is from J. Whitcut, *Learning with LDOCE*, Longman, 1979. Examples 48b and
    48c are from E. Kirkpatrick, *op. cit.* (A newer workbook to accompany the latest edition of
    the LDOCE is now available, by J. McAlpin.)
9. Example 49a is from V. Black, M. McNorton, A. Maldares and S. Parker, *Fast Forward
    Resource Book*, Oxford University Press, 1986; Example 49b is from P. Harvey and C. Walker,
    Way Ahead (3), Penguin, 1986.
10. Example 50 and succeeding text is from M. Wallace, *Teaching Vocabulary*, Heinemann, 1982.
11. Example 51a is from J. Whitcut *op. cit.*; Example 51b is from D. Sim and B. Laufer-Dvorkin,
    Vocabulary Development, Collins ELT, 1984.
12. Example 52a is from R. Belgrave, *Way Ahead (2)*, Penguin, 1986; Example 52b is from J.
    Morgan and M. Rinvolucri, *Vocabulary*, Oxford University Press, 1986.
13. Examples 53a and 53b are from D. Sim and B. Laufer-Dvorkin, *op. cit.*; Example 53c is from
    P. Viney, *Streamline English Directions*, Oxford University Press, 1985.

14. Example 53d is from M. Winter, *Working with Your 2000 Word Dictionary*, Harrap, 1981.
15. Examples 54a–f from D. Sim and V. Laufer-Dvorkin, *Vocabulary Development*, Collins 1984 (54a); P. Aston, 'Activity book' for *Up the Creek*, in T. Hedge, *Using Readers in Language Teaching*, Macmillan, 1985 (54b); P. Viney, *op. cit.* (54c); V. Black *et al., op. cit* (54d); J. Morgan and M. Rinvolucri, *Vocabulary*, Oxford University Press, 1986 (54e); and R. Gairns and S. Redman, *op. cit.* (54f).
16. Examples 55a–e from E. Kirkatrick, *op. cit.* (55a); P. Viney, *op. cit.* (55b); P. Harvey and C. Walker, *op. cit.* (55c); D. Sim and B. Laufer-Dvorkin, *op. cit* (55d); and J. Morgan and M. Rinvolucri, *Learning English Words*, Pilgrims, 1980 (55e).
17. Examples 56a and 56b from J. Whitcut, *op. cit.*
18. Examples 57a–c from C. Grainger and D. Beaumont, *New Generation (1)*, Heinemann 1986 (57a); J. Harmer, *Meridian Activity Book (1)*, Longman, 1985 (57b); and P. Harvey and C. Walker, *op. cit.* (57c).
19. Examples 58a–c from V. Black *et al., op. cit* (58a); R. Belgrave, *op. cit* (58b); and P. Harvey and C. Walker, *op. cit.* (58c).
20. *Word and letter games*
    (a) 'Scrabble' is made by Selchow & Righter Co., Bay Shore, New York 11706, USA, and J.W. Spear & Sons Ltd, Enfield, Middlesex, UK.
    (b) Crossword Dice devised by Stephen Leslie for Onsworld's Jackpot Dice Series, Onsworld Ltd.
    (c) Sound/spelling games such as 'Syllable Snap and Rummy' are available from Taskmaster Ltd, Morris Road, Leicester LE2 6BR.
    (d) Learning Development Aids (LDA), Duke Street, Wisbech, Cambs. PE13 2AE publish a pack of 'Phonic Reference Cards' with teachers' notes for quick reference, if a list of words displaying a particular sound is needed, e.g. there's a card on 'silent b' including 'lamb', 'comb', 'plumber', etc.
    (e) 'Boggle' is made by Palitoy, CPG Products Corp., Minneapolis, Minn., USA, or in the UK at Coalville, Leicester.
    (f) 'Crossword' dice game and 'Hangman' are made by MB Games (Milton Bradley Ltd) under Berne University Copyright Convention.
    (g) Lexicon letter game is made by Waddington Games Ltd, UK.
    (h) Debden Suffix Changing Cards by K. Hadley and Cromwell Word Meaning Activities by John Baguley are both available from Philip and Tacey Ltd, North Way, Andover, Hants.
    (i) There are many computer packages designed to help learners with spelling problems, such as 'Vocab' from Wida Software Ltd, 2 Nicholas Gardens, London W5 5HY.
21. T. Hedge, *op. cit.*
22. Example 59a is from J. Whitcut, *op. cit.*
23. C. E. Ott, D. C. Butler, R. S. Blake and J. P. Ball, 'The effect of interactive image elaboration on the acquisition of foreign language vocabulary', *Language Learning* 1973, **23(2)**: 197–206.
24. Example 59b is from J. Morgan and M. Rinvolucri, *op. cit.*
25. D. Summers, 'The role of dictionaries in language learning' in R. Carter and M. McCarthy, *Vocabulary and Language Teaching*, Longman, 1988.
26. Picture or photo dictionaries, such as the *Longman Photo Dictionary*, and simple monolingual dictionaries, such as the *Harrap 2000 Word Dictionary*, can help the transition.
27. I am thinking especially of the revised *Longman Dictionary of Contemporary English*, and of the *Collins Cobuild Dictionary*.
28. For a more detailed treatment of learner's dictionaries see M. P. Jain, 'On meaning in the foreign learner's dictionary', *Applied Linguistics*, vol. II, no. 3.
29. See D. Summers, *op. cit.*
30. From *The Times*, the *Daily Mail, The Guardian* and *Today*, Wed. 5 April 1989.
31. Extracts taken from the *Collins Cobuild English Language Dictionary*, Collins ELT, 1987.

Chapter 5

Vocabulary in Discourse

In this final chapter I want to suggest ways of encouraging learners to guess meaning from context. All that has been offered so far is in fact only the beginning – we have merely taken vocabulary out of context and sensitised our learners to some ideas about what it means to know a word. Ultimately, they will have to discover meanings without our help, and we must equip them to do this.

It may take considerable time for our foreign learners to make the leap from facility in working through vocabulary exercises to facility in deciphering the meaning of unknown items in connected discourse of some length, either spoken or written.[1]

5.1 The wider context: Spoken discourse

Kennedy and Bolitho[2] draw attention to the importance for ESP/EAP learners of training in listening to lectures. Apart from non-verbal cues like gesture and facial expression, which can be taught only through the use of videotaped lectures, there are other cues, like intonation and pausing, and signalling devices like *right, well, so*, which indicate the beginnings and endings of sections in the discourse. Repetitions in the form of synonyms or paraphrase, backtracking and summarising occur as part of the redundancy associated with the spoken mode. Thus if we wish to further our learners' oral/aural skills, we must not overlook the pragmatic aspect of vocabulary.

Three very important areas here are discourse organisers, emphasisers and downgraders, terms which I shall define and explain in turn (all examples from Cobuild corpora).

5.1.1 The discourse organiser

This is a word or words which help(s) an audience to understand what has just been said or is about to be said by setting up a framework for rhetorical organisation within which your message is contained. It may be one of four types:

(a) It may focus attention on what will follow, e.g.:
    'I am limiting the *following* observations to the Christian faith.'
    'There are *several reasons* for this...*First*...'
    '*Look*...I want to go to Europe for six months.'
(b) It may sum up or focus on what has just been said, e.g.:
    '*That then*, is the basis for wheat bread.'
    '*To recapitulate*, there are three main approaches...'

'*Thus it was* that around the turn of the century, my father...'
'*The upshot of it all* was that we couldn't go.'
(c) It may mark a boundary, bridge or resting point between what has just been said and what is to follow, e.g.:
'*I would like now to switch* to quite a different area.'
'*Turning* to your new job, you start in August is that right?'
'*The other thing* of course is that people never take him seriously.'
(d) It may focus attention on important points of what is being said, e.g.:
'*The fact of the matter is*, Cynthia said she'd meet me...'
'*I want to make it clear* that...'
'*Far and away the most important aspect* is...'

5.1.2 The downgrader

This is a word or words used to modify what is said so as to make it more acceptable to the audience. It may be one of three types:

(a) It may appear as a preface, before the blow to be softened, e.g.:
'*I know it's very wrong of me* but...'
'*I don't know about you*, but...'
'*I can't help thinking that*...'
(b) It may appear after the blow to be softened, e.g.:
'I'd like to marry Mr Barter, *in a way*.'
'We had a very bad year last year, *I'm afraid to say*.'
'She's quite sweet, Sheila, *if you like the style*.'
(c) It may occur as an integral part of an utterance, often several at once, e.g.:
'I think you are *perhaps* exaggerating *slightly*.'
'I don't say that's *necessarily* a good thing.'
'The Baltic exits were *to all intents and purposes* in Soviet hands.'

5.1.3 The emphasiser

This is most often an adjective or adverb, a word or words used t⌐
point being made. It may be any of the following:

(a) A formula, fixed expression, or with restri
'*And I for one* am going to look forward to
'I'll say *here and now* that I don't believe in
'He could*n't* spell *to save his life*.'
'I was *insanely jealous* of his IQ.'
'I'm scared, *scared stiff*.'
(b) A simile, e.g.:
'As tough as old boots.'
'As pleased as Punch.'

(c) With distinct positive or negative bias, e.g.:

 'Her room is a *hopeless* muddle.'

 'My father was *bitterly* disappointed.'   negative

 'A piece of *blatant* egotism.'

 '*Sheer* delight.'

 'A *runaway* success.'   positive

 '*Rapturous* applause'

Learners can also be shown more simple ways of achieving emphasis, such as repetition of the important lexical item, e.g.:

'The Germans are *streets* and *streets* ahead of us...'

'She wants to *talk* and *talk*...'

'He sits for *hour* after *hour*, *week* after *week, year* after *year*.'

or the use of an auxiliary verb, e.g.:

'I *do* believe...';   'He *will* insist.'

It will be seen that many of the above items, when in use, have little if any semantic content, so the only way to teach their correct use is to explain them in terms of discourse function.

For help with listening to lectures, learners could be taught to note down, say, the 'emphasisers' used in a selected extract, choosing from a set of alternatives the ones which were actually used. Note-taking exercises often encourage learners to focus on content but, paradoxically, by concentrating on forms of words instead, learners are enabled to decode meaning. Exercises on recognition of 'downgraders' and 'emphasisers', for example, are invaluable in helping learners to separate fact from lecturer's opinion − a necessary skill for foreigners who are pursuing academic study in Britain.

5.2 Prosody

Prosody is another area which should be familiarised to learners. Firstly, stress patterns which obtain for words in isolation may change in connected speech. One way of marking stress in sentences is this one (Example 60):

EXAMPLE 60[3]

Say these sentences with the correct stress:
1. **Two sing**les to **Rug**by, **please**.
 What time is the **next train** to **Cam**bridge, **please**?
 There's a di**rect train** at **six forty**.
 Which platform?
 w would you **like** it?
 orry, I **don't** under**stand**. Could you speak more **slow**ly?

Another (Example 61) appears in Brazil (1985) and shows clearly how 'the precise location of prominent syllables is automatically adjusted to bring them as near the beginning and end of the tonic segment as possible'. (Upper case indicates strong stress, upper case and underscore together indicate nucleus.).

EXAMPLE 61[4]

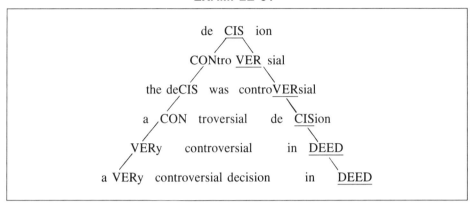

Learners can be given a text and asked to underline one − or at most two − word(s) in each sentence which they think to be the most important. The learners then read the text aloud, taking care to make only those words prominent, by stressing them. This exercise has the effect of speeding up reading, leading to a more natural use of weak forms. The learners could then listen to a native speaker reading the identical text, underlining the prominent syllables, and checking with their own. In this way, the communicative value of prominence, i.e. its role in conveying meaning, is made clear.

Brazil has noted that English speakers use raised pitch, as well as prominence, to emphasise what is new in the discourse, especially where it contrasts with expectations:

EXAMPLE 62[5]

> A: I thought his name was John.
>
> B: It ^{IS} John.
>
> A: So the food was quite reasonable then.
>
> B: On the contrary. It was dis^{GUS}ting.
> (Superscript denotes raised pitch.)

Brazil uses the term 'key' when referring to a raising or lowering of pitch, and it is his notions of 'prominence' and 'key' which McCarthy feels have importance for the teaching of vocabulary in the context of interaction. In conversation, one speaker often repeats what the other has said, but in non-identical form: he relexicalises (i.e. substitutes another word, sometimes involving rephrasing):

EXAMPLE 63[6]

A: Have you HEARD? Joe SMITH's got a new JOB. He's LEAVing.
B: Well I NEVer though HE'd go.

A: ...but I had TROUBLE GETting my PAPers. I eVENtually got a work permit
after about a FIVE month deLAY.

A: PEOPle just don't WORK Saturday MORnings ofFIcially in LONdon.
B: Does HE come in on Saturdays?
(Upper case denotes prominent, i.e. stressed syllables.)

In the above example, the prominent, high-pitched 'leave' is equivalent to the non-prominent, low-pitched 'go'. 'Papers' is equivalent to 'work permit', and 'work' equivalent to 'come in'. They are *equivalent*, not *semantically identical*. Equivalence is thus a kind of synonymy; and an opposing value, analogous to antonymy, would be indicated by prominence and high key (raised pitch):

EXAMPLE 64

A: Lovely day, isn't it?
B: Yes, ^{BEAU}tiful.
(Superscript denotes raised pitch.)

As a classroom exercise in discrimination, learners could listen to a recording of two-line dialogues, indicating whether speaker B is expressing equivalent value (synonymy) or opposing value (antonymy):

EXAMPLE 65

(a) A: Dreadful day, isn't it?
    B: Yes, awful. (awful = dreadful)
(b) A: Is he good at football?
    B: Yes, he's $^{NOT\ BAD}$. (not bad > good)
(c) A: Have you given up the fags?
    B. Yes, I never ^{TOUCH} them now. (never touch > give up)

The same material could be used as an exercise in production, where only A's part is given and learners are asked to supply plausible responses. In the case of (a) above, these might include 'Yes it is' (= dreadful), 'Yes, very' (= dreadful), '^{GHAST}ly' (> dreadful).

McCarthy[7] believes that quite subtle functions are fulfilled by varying lexical choice within and over turn boundaries, and that we should help out learners by presenting vocabulary in discourse contexts which illustrate these functions. Since the management of interaction involves *lexical* as well as *grammatical* skills, a 'lexical syllabus' which includes patterns of lexical relations taken from actual data would counterbalance the traditional emphasis on decontextualised meaning.

Tone is another feature of intonation to listen for because new information is always given with falling tone. Rising tones are used when referring to knowledge which the speaker shares with his hearer. Students could be asked to listen to a recorded extract and mark the falling tones:

EXAMPLE 66[8]

When I've prepared my lecture, if there's any time left, I shall go into town, and

after that it will depend on the weather. Perhaps I shall play tennis if it's fit and

if there's anyone around. Otherwise I'll write some letters.

They could then write a report based on their marked transcript, including only information conveyed in falling tones. A pre-task activity for the report-writing would be to check in pairs or in groups whether they had a consensus on the positioning of falling tones, and to clarify the meaning of any unknown lexis conveyed in these falling tones. In this way, learners would be sensitised to the fact that they do not have to note everything said in a lecture, but should concentrate on what the speaker wants to communicate to the audience. This will be delivered with a falling intonation.

5.3 The wider context: Written discourse

Bensoussan and Laufer[9] have noted that L2 learners do not pay attention to contextual clues when reading, but rely on 'preconceived notions' about word meanings. Strategies they isolate include the following:

1. Appropriate guess, e.g. *profound* for *important*.
2. Mistranslating an idiom, or translating it word for word, e.g. *outline* as *out of line*.
3. A wild guess, or wrong polyseme (e.g. *bill* (receipt) for *bill* (beak)).
4. An inappropriate guess, correct in grammar but wrong in meaning.
5. Ignoring the word completely.

Learners can be helped to guess meaning from context by using gapped texts — either traditional or modified cloze — or perhaps by using nonsense words with English affixes, as in this example which I made for a group of lower intermediate students:

EXAMPLE 67

'Last Saturday I went WUGGLING in Sheffield. I wanted to buy some WUGGLES for my family for Christmas.

First I went to a clothes shop and bought a WUGGLE for my father. I chose a furry one with flaps to keep his ears warm.

Next I went to choose some WUGGLERY for my sister. I found a beautiful locket of silver with a matching chain.

I do hope my family will be WUGGLY when they see what I have bought.'

The first two nonsense items are easily guessed with a little cross-cultural knowledge if the word *buy* is taken into account, but the third cannot be accurately guessed until the whole of the following sentence has been read and digested. The fourth item is the most difficult, and in my class necessitated the use of the dictionary for the item *locket* in most cases, and for *chain* in some. The final item was within the grasp of all the students and boosted confidence in guessing.

We can also ask learners to underline certain items in a given text and to guess what they mean without using a dictionary, to see what strategies come to light. The following exercise (Example 68) involves underlining items in the text and then finding antonyms for them, again from the text, thus revealing how antonymy works in context:

EXAMPLE 68[10]

Below are six words and phrases from the text (line references are in brackets). For each one, find in the text a word of opposite meaning and write it in the appropriate space.

1. increase (2)   *diminish*   4. desert (i)   _____

2. inconvenient (7)   _____   5. fixity (18)   _____

3. abolish (7)   _____   6. be retained (22) _____

Multiple choice can be used to narrow the focus in guessing, as in Example 69, which also shows how meaning can be guessed and demonstrated via visual means; and in Example 70:

EXAMPLE 69[11]

5.2 How well can you guess the meaning of the words you do not know?

Work with a partner and try to answer the following questions. You can probably guess by simply looking at the sentence in which a word appears.

Paragraph 1 (Haggard . . .)
The three words used to describe Juliane (*haggard, bruised, dazed*) suggest
☐ happiness.
☐ shock.
☐ surprise.

In the paragraph, find synonyms for:
● a difficult time.
● an aeroplane.
● to be saved.
● the jungle.
Below (line 4) means ☐ above.
☐ near.
☐ under.

Paragraph 6 (Juliane first heard. . .)
screened (line 2) means
☐ showed.
☐ reflected.
☐ hid.

Find four words showing that Juliane is a little hurt.

Paragraph 7 (Though probably suffering . . .)
Find an expression meaning the same thing as 'to be sure to'.

Paragraph 8 (she began. . .)
A *swamp* is ☐ hard ground.
☐ grass.
☐ soft wet land.
To *stumble* means ☐ to run.
☐ to walk with difficulty.
☐ to walk quickly.

Paragraph 11 (After the first three days . . .)
You *shiver* when you are ☐ thirsty.
☐ cold.
☐ hot.

Paragraph 13 (Four days after the crash. . .)
Find a word which means 'to move with difficulty'. What would a 'winding river' look like? Draw a line to show this.

EXAMPLE 70[12]

Instructions. This exercise will help to direct your attention to the kind of information that a context may give you. In the exercise there are three sentences, each one adding a little more information. Each sentence has three possible definitions of the nonsense word. On the basis of information in the sentence, decide if the definition is improbable, possible or probable. Write one of these words on the line for each definition.
1. We had a whoosis.
a tropical fish _____
an egg beater _____
a leather suitcase _____

2. We had a whoosis, but the handle broke.
   a tropical fish   _____
   an egg beater   _____
   a leather suitcase   _____
3. We had a whoosis, but the handle broke, so we
   had to beat the eggs with a fork.
   a tropical fish   _____
   an egg beater   _____
   a leather suitcase   _____

Finally, here is an example which shows how L1 can be exploited for guessing words in context:

EXAMPLE 71[13]

This exercise type is for students who share the same mother tongue.

Take an English text your students will find gripping and translate it into their mother tongue. Leave one word per sentence or so in English. Choose words that can be guessed fairly accurately from the sentence context. Choose words that are repeated in the text.

Pick a fairly long text that the students can work on for a few minutes per session over several weeks. Leave progressively more of the text in English but do not be tempted to put too much in English too soon, or the students will go too slowly and the reading will be heavy.

The Barbarians come in the night...

When the telephone kudunisi in the middle of the night, something unusual is happening. Just such a tilefonima woke me up at dawn on the 21st of April 1967. From the other end tis gramis the journalist, George Papachristophilou told me in a trembling voice:

'There's been a coup — there are tanks everywhere and they're surrounding everything — leave your spiti...'

'Are you serious? I rotisa him.'

'Ne, I tell you, I can see rifles, machine-guns, helmets, stratiotes, get out while you can!'

I put down the tilefono and stayed silent for some seconds. Then I began dialling arithmus. All grames to the centre had been cut off...

The task of deciphering the meaning of unfamiliar items embedded in authentic English discourse is indeed a daunting one for foreign learners. It is hoped that the ideas and activities presented in this volume will enable teachers to take their students some way towards that final goal.

5.4 Tasks

Group Tasks

1. Look at the section on 'downgraders' in this chapter. For each situation below, you are given a bald statement to say as part of a dialogue. Discuss how you could *add* to this statement, without changing any of the words within it, so as to 'soften the blow':

    Situation 1:   A very dear friend of yours has just bought some new clothes and is very pleased with them. You don't like them at all.

    Your friend: How do you like my new outfit? It's the first time I've worn it!

    You: I think it's awful.

    Situation 2:   You are supposed to meet an old friend tonight at the cinema but you now realise you have overlooked a previous engagement. You meet by chance in the street during the afteroon.

    Your old friend: Well hello there! I'm really looking forward to tonight!

    You: I can't come.

    Situation 3:   Your boss wants to have an 'open day' to show the kind of work done in the establishment in which you work. You have no wish to run it. On the contrary, you have told your boss that you will only do so if no one else wants to take it on.

    Your boss: You said you would get your department to organise it.

    You: No I didn't.

    Situation 4:   A mutual colleague has been chosen to lead a team, which includes you and your friend, on a new work project. You do not share the same opinion as your friend about this colleague, but you want to avoid an argument.

    Your friend: S/he's absolutely impossible to work with, and what's more s/he's just plain incompetent.

    You: I think s/he's the ideal person for the job.

2. Here are some ways speakers have used to emphasise what they are saying. Look again at the section on 'emphasisers' in this chapter and discuss other words they could have used to achieve the same effect, e.g.:

    THERE WAS *QUITE A* LARGE INPUT.

    Possible alternatives: The amount of input was quite something.

    There was a fair size of input.

    There was a pretty large input.

    (a) But it's inevitable, *isn't it*?
    (b) This is a *very* important question.
    (c) We try to make our voice heard *as loudly as possible*.
    (d) *Only a* handful of people know we exist.

(e) What I'm *really* concerned about is that we should appeal to everyone.
(f) Well, there *are* training units nationally, but not necessarily locally.
(g) Most of us *thoroughly* enjoy our work.
(The 'emphasiser' has been italicised for you in each case, and you should replace it with another of your own.)

3. This is an activity in guessing words from context, and each member of your group must begin by doing the task alone. After you have read each sentence, write down your first idea about what 'it' might be. Don't read the next sentence until you have recorded your idea about the previous one in the space provided. When you have completed all six spaces, discuss with others in your group how their ideas differed from yours, and why:

(a) Dear Martin! How sweet of him to send it to her.   *'it'* = _____
(b) Fancy remembering her favourite colour.
     It looked so beautiful in the sunlight.   *'it'* = _____
(c) She took it out of its box and held it up to the window. *'it'* = _____
(d) The silver strands sparkled and shone.   *'it'* = _____
(e) Then she brushed it carefully.   *'it'* = _____
(f) She would wear it to the party tonight,
     and no-one would recognise her.   *'it'* = _____

Self-assessed tasks

1. We have said that discourse organisers can be classified into three types: (a) those that focus on what will follow; (b) those that sum up or focus on what has been said; and (c) those that form a boundary, bridge or resting place between what has been said and what will come next. Look at the discourse organisers which have been underlined for you in the following passage,[14] and classify them according to the three types:

> 'Can you tell me what you mean by "stress"?'
> 'What I mean by "stress" is when pressure exceeds an individual's ability to cope with it. *In other words*, pressure is usually fairly healthy, it stimulates people to action, but when that pressure gets to the point that you get maladaptive behaviour in one form or another, either social behaviour that's not appropriate, or health behaviour, it affects your health, your relationships, you marriage, then I think we're moving from pressure into stress.'
> 'I see. And how does stress counselling work?'
> '*I think it's very important that* management should know the kind of pressures involved for the people they are employing and should do something to help. Stress counselling is *nothing more than* a service made available by trained staff whereby any member of staff can go in if they have a problem. *Now* the problem does not have to be a work related problem. The object of that is, if an individual is having a problem in his marriage, that person is going to walk into work and that problem's not going to go away, it's going to affect him or her at work. *So basically* the service really allows an individual to go for help, somebody to talk to. It may be a long-term problem or a legal problem that requires more expertise, in which case that person can then be referred.'
> 'How does this service differ from others already in existence?'

'*OK. What we've done is* we've carried out a systematic evaluation and we've found substantial drops in anxiety levels, depression levels and psychosomatic symptoms. *But more interesting than that is* that we looked at what happened in the workplace. These counsellors are not only concerned with the individual but with the organisation. And we found between a 50 and 60 per cent decline in sickness absence over a six-month period. *So* it'll save the organisation quite a lot of money.'

2. Remember that speakers use a falling tone when they are giving new information. Mark where you think falling tones would be appropriate in the passage below. Read it aloud according to your markings to check that it sounds good. Now, using the marked words as your main points, summarise the passage in not more than seventy-five words. Check with the key.

'Well I don't think the post-elementary student, the archetypal post-elementary student, exists. The students who need post-elementary help, as with all post-elementary students, should be defined in terms of their need, and their own feeling that they want help, at a level which is not being met in the general English classes. In general terms, it's somebody who in everyday situations, in ordinary social conversation, you would not think had any need to go to English classes. They're perfectly capable of carrying out the normal things like going shopping, going to the doctor, having a social evening round at your house — all of these things they can handle perfectly competently. But it's when things go wrong, or when they're under stress, that the language problems start to emerge.'

3. Against each of the following words, write the first synonym (word or phrase) which comes to mind. Now substitute your own words or phrases into the text in the Key for this question, in place of the originals. Does the text still make sense?

(a) branch   _____

(b) tear   _____

(c) bill   _____

(d) invalid   _____

(e) refuse   _____

(f) desert   _____

Notes and references

1 N. Bullard, 'Word based perception: A handicap in second language acquisition', *ELTJ* January 1985, **39/1**: 28−32.
2. C. Kennedy and R. Bolitho, *English for Specific Purposes*, Macmillan, 1984.
3. Example 60 is from M. Swan and C. Walter, *The Cambridge English Course I*, Practice Book, Cambridge University Press, 1984.
4. Example 61 is from D. Brazil, *The Communicative Value of Intonation in English*, ELR, University of Birmingham, 1985.
5. D. Brazil, *op. cit*. In her book *Intonation in Context* (Cambridge, 1988), Barbara Bradford has adapted Brazil's ideas for use with upper intermediate and advanced learners of English.
6. Example 63 is from M. McCarthy, 'Some vocabulary patterns in conversation' in *Vocabulary and Language Teaching*, Longman, 1988.
7. *Ibid*.

8. Example 66 is from D. Brazil, *op. cit.*
9. M. Bensoussan and B. Laufer, 'Lexical guessing in context in EFL reading comprehension', *Journal of Research in Reading* 1984, **i(1)**: 15−32. Computer packages based on cloze procedure help learners with inferencing skills. One such is 'Clozemaster', available from Wida Software Ltd, 2 Nicholas Gardens, London W5 5HY.
10. Example 68 is from D. Sim and B. Laufer-Dvorkin, *op. cit.*
11. Example 69 is from F. Grellet, A. Maley and W. Welsing, *Quartet Students' Book I*, Oxford University Press, 1982.
12. Example 70 is from J. Honeyfield, 'Word frequency and the importance of context in vocabulary learning', *RELC Journal* 1977, **8(2)**: 35−42.
13. Example 71 is from J. Morgan and M. Rinvolucri, *Learning English Words*, Pilgrims, 1980.
14. Adapted from 'Medicine now', BBC Radio 4, 5 April 1989.

Appendix

Key to Self-Assessed Tasks

Chapter 1

1. well
   actually
   whether
   certainly
   obviously
   absolutely
   whatever
   exactly

2.

Formal	Less Formal
He passed away	He kicked the bucket
Could I ask you to make a little less noise?	Put a sock in it
You are requested to remain seated	Don't move
I advise you to buy the next size up	I should get a bigger one if I were you
There was torrential rain	It was absolutely bucketing down

3.

Sports	Housework	Hobbies
cycling jogging walking in the mountains	cleaning floors washing dishes making beds	sewing stamp collecting bird watching

The chart above gives one possibility. You will perhaps have seen that the classification is not always clear-cut: sewing may be a hobby for some, but housework for others; perhaps you might class some sports as hobbies? Did you devise other headings, such as 'outdoor activities', 'women's work'?

4. NOUN: -tion, -ment, -ness
    VERB: -ic, -ous, -ful, -ive, -al
    But what about 'spoonful', 'directive', 'rhetoric'? In English new nouns are being formed almost daily from adjectives. I recently heard a document referred to as 'a glossy'!

5. 'Cough'/'touch' and 'bother'/'another' cannot rhyme because of the middle vowel, ɒ and ʌ respectively. 'A'rithmetic'/'anaes'thetic' cannot rhyme because of different stress pattern. The rest can.

6. (a) Learning.
    (b) Learning.
    (c) Acquisition.
    (d) Learning.
    (e) Acquisition.

    Notice that in the 'learning' examples the teacher focuses the learners' attention on the new item by initiating a word search, then consolidating by means of repetition and perhaps written reinforcement. In the 'acquisition' examples the focus is not on the vocabulary item itself, but on the wider meaning of the discourse as a whole. There may well be repetition, but this is student-generated; the teacher does not dwell on the item, and thereby maintains fluency.

Chapter 2

1. (a) Sound and spelling.
    (b) Collocation.
    (c) Register.
    (d) Morphology.
    (e) L1 equivalent.

2. (a) Post-familiarisation, written stimulus (later oral/aural).
    (b) Pre-familiarisation, non-verbal stimulus.
    (c) Pre-familiarisation, oral/aural stimulus (but although no picture is shown, there is strong visual imagery here).
    (d) Post-familiarisation, oral/aural stimulus (pictures were in fact used, but only indirectly for the item concerned).

Chapter 3

1. (a) 1. Posing a direct question.
    (b) 3. Rising intonation (this should be obvious from the question mark).
    (c) 2. Using a tag.

2. (a) 6. Attending to both acoustic and semantic aspects.
    (b) 5. Giving more than one synonym, paraphrase or example. (1. Using a phrase
            such as 'that means' is also present, but prompted by a student.)
    (c) 4. Eliciting a number of repetitions of the items. (Not 6. because semantic aspect
            is not attended to.)

Chapter 4

1. Article from *The Times*, 5 April 1989
    The widow of Mr Colin Townsley, the fireman who died in the King's Cross fire,
    was awarded damages of £250,000 in the High Court yesterday. The award to Mrs
    Linda Townsley, which was approved by Mr Justice Michael Davies, is a record for
    a fireman killed on duty. Part of the award was made in respect of the "minutes of
    terror" the senior fireman suffered when he collapsed from the fumes and was waiting
    to be enveloped by the fireball that killed a total of 31 people. Mr Benet Hytner QC,
    for Mrs Townsley, paid tribute to the man who had "died a hero's death".

    (Reproduced by kind permission of Times Newspapers Ltd)

    Article from *Today*, 5 April 1989
    The widow of King's Cross fireman Colin Townsley was awarded £250,000 damages
    yesterday. Mrs Linda Townsley looked strained and repeatedly turned her wedding
    ring as the High Court heard how her husband "died a hero's death" in the 1987
    Tube inferno. As toxic smoke filled the Underground Station he turned back from
    a chance to escape to help a badly burned woman. Station Officer Townsend "suffered
    some minutes of terror of impending death" as he suffocated in a tunnel, said Benet
    Hytner QC.

    (Reproduced by kind permission of *Today*)

    Article from the *Daily Mail*, 5 April 1989
    The widow of King's Cross hero fireman Colin Townsley finally received £250,000
    damages from London Underground yesterday. Mrs Linda Townsley took her case
    to the High Court to force a settlement for the November 1987 tragedy in which 31
    died. After the hearing in London her solicitor, Mr Andrew Dismore, strongly criticised
    the Underground for 'intransigence' which he said had caused Mrs Townsley many
    months of worry and uncertainty. "London Underground held out to the last minute
    – the negotiations were concluded only 3 weeks ago" he said.

    (Reproduced by kind permission of the *Daily Mail*)

The article from *The Times* is the most formal and most detached: notice the lack of emotive language and predominance of passive constructions ('was awarded', 'was approved', 'was made'). Any emotive language used is clearly spoken by those involved in the trial, not necessarily endorsed by the writer.

The article from *Today* is still quite formal, with passive constructions, but notice 'loaded' vocabulary such as 'looked strained', 'inferno', 'suffocated', and the active verb 'turned back'. There is still some effort to contain exaggeration and subjectivity by use of quotation marks, however.

The article from the *Daily Mail* is clearly written from a stance which sympathises with Mrs Townsley in her efforts to speed up justice and obtain money from London Underground. Notice the use of the strictly unnecessary 'finally' and the violence of 'forced' and 'strongly criticised'. We are a long way here from the mere reporting of facts.

2. Leila started attending her secondary school in September. After two to three weeks, the first-year children were assessed and graded. Leila's reading age was assessed as thirteen years, and her spelling age, fifteen years. She was consequently allocated to a class in the top band, where she had none of her former classmates from primary school, and was therefore separated from her close friends. Leila was very outspoken and articulate and particularly enjoyed contributing to class discussions. She found that she was the only girl to do so. I believe that many of the boys, particularly the dominant group, saw this as a threat to their control. The boys' response to behaviour they considered competitive was to attempt to intimidate Leila with racist and sexist abuse, threats and physical violence. Other girls avoided this attention by keeping quiet.

(Adapted from *Just a Bunch of Girls* by Gaby Weiner (ed.),
Oxford University Press, 1985.

3. (a) goes with (ii).
    (b) goes with (iii).
    (c) goes with (iv).
    (d) goes with (v).
    (e) goes with (i).
    (f) goes with (vii).
    (g) goes with (vi).

4. (a) Tulip.
    (b) Cottage.
    (c) Violence.
    (d) Affection.

Chapter 5

1. (a) type organisers: I think it's very important that...
   ...nothing more than...
   What we've done is...
   But more interesting than that is...

   (b) type organisers: In other words...
   So basically...
   So...

   (c) type organisers: Now...
   OK...

2. The falling tones are on:

   exists

   need (1st time it appears)

   classes

   need (2nd time it appears)

   competently

   wrong

   stress

   emerge

   So the summary would read something like this:

   > An archetypal post-elementary learner doesn't *exist*, except as defined in terms of a type of *need* not met in general English *classes*. This *need* for English tuition is not normally evident, because these students manage quite *competently* in most situations. It's only when things go *wrong*, or when the learner is under *stress*, that language problems *emerge*.

   (Remember that this is only *one* way of saying the passage. You may have stressed different words. Check with a teacher/friend whether they would still be correct.)

3.

   > Was that the 'phone? Not again! Mary went into the hall and picked up the receiver with shaking hand:
   > 'Hello.'
   > 'Good morning, Swann's, Retford *branch* here.'
   > 'Oh yes.'
   > 'I'm afraid the cheque you gave us in settlement of our *bill* for £200 is *invalid*. The bank *refuse* to pay it.'
   > 'Oh, I'm terribly sorry. I'll contact them right away.'
   > 'Thank you, madam.'
   > She sank into a chair. Her usual brisk, confident manner had begun to *desert* her. A *tear* formed in the corner of her eye and slowly descended her ashen-white cheek.